PROXIMITIES OF CALVARY

AUTHOR OF:

"From Feet to Fathoms"
"Lord, I Believe"
"A Greater than Solomon"
"A Grand-Canyon of Resurrection Realities"
"Whirlwinds of God"
"Lee Lines"
"Pickings"
"The Name Above Every Name"
"The Blood of Jesus Christ"
"Buried and Alive"
"Treasurers of the Snow"
"One Plus God"
"Glory Today for Conquest Tomorrow"
"Calvary"

Proximities of Calvary

By

ROBERT G. LEE, D.D., LL.D., LITT.D.

Pastor of
Bellevue Baptist Church
Memphis, Tenn.

Robert G. Lee SERMONIC LIBRARY

CHRIST FOR THE WORLD PUBLISHERS
Post Office Box 3428 — 1209 W. 29th St.
Orlando, Florida 32802

First Printing, 1940
Second Printing, 1981
3RD PRINTING, 1985

Printed by Permission

Printed in the United States of America
DANIELS PUBLISHING COMPANY
1209 - 29th Street
Orlando, Florida 32805

DEDICATION

To our Bellevue office workers:—

MISS RUTH CALVERT, *Pastor's Secretary*
MISS LETTY WILKINSON, *Financial Secretary*
MRS. STANLEY M. ARMSTRONG, *Director of Young Peoples work*
MRS. TOM CONE, *Sunday School Secretary*

To These
Four Christian Women—

Sweet in spirit, devoted in duty, loyal in word and deed, faithful in service, helpful in friendship, Christlike in conduct,

This book is gratefully dedicated
by
THE AUTHOR

CONTENTS

CHAPTER I

THAT LAST WEEK

THE last week of the public ministry of our Lord Jesus on this sin-smitten, sin-saddened earth is the climax of the history of the world. No other week that has passed beyond recall into the tomb of Time is like it. No other week that shall ever come, by the will of God, from the womb of Time can be like it. The vast importance of that week is shown in the space devoted to it by the writers of the Gospels—writers who wrote by the Holy Spirit. One-third of Matthew's Gospel relates to events within one week of the end of Christ's public ministry. So also is such true with two-fifths of Mark's Gospel. Moreover, one-fourth of Luke's Gospel records events within one week of the end. Not only so. One-half of John's Gospel points intensely to events within one week of the end. And of John's twenty-one chapters, the last nine chapters are taken up with events within one week of the end of that public ministry which has bannered all the lands with love and perfumed the stifling air of continents. Only two of the Gospel writers tell at any length of his temptation experience—Matthew and Luke. Only two of the Gospel writers recite Christ's sermon on the Mount—Matthew and Luke. But all enlarge on the tragedy and triumph of his death.

Now, in entering the vast domains of that week and in considering the stupendous events thereof, we enter holy white sanctuaries where only irreverent and ungrateful men and women can stand without humbly and worshipfully taking their shoes from off their feet. In journeying through the tangled woods of that week we are amazed as, with eyes anointed with spiritual salve, we behold the wonders--the heart-rending, the mind-startling, the soul-inspiring wonders—of that week. If we have eyes to see, if we have ears to hear, if we have hearts to understand, we shall find ourselves following highways and bypaths of tragedies as well as bypaths and highways of triumph.

Looking upon that week as a continent, considering its boundaries and its areas, its reach toward the past, its reach toward the future, its reach downward, its reach upward, its reach outward, its reach inward to the very soul of mankind, we shall see lakes of unquenchable fire and sulphurous brimstone surrounded with precipitous shores of black and beetling crags over whose surface beat eternal storms. We shall feel nauseous revulsions as we smell the fumes from sulphurous torches held in the hands of fiends as they stumble and fall and howl in pits and chasms and black corners—and in lighted streets. We shall stand dazed as we hear the "unfettered thunders of God" as hell's infernal drums "roll the eternal bass in hell's uproar, and beat time to the ceaseless groans of the lost." We shall discover islands whose rocks and mountains and fields are tumbled into anarchy. We shall see also islands in summer seas where blushing flowers and nodding trees make miniature Paradises. We shall shudder as we gaze understandingly into "stinking caves inhabited with fiends and gnashing ghosts." We shall shudderingly behold black crags where "the ravens of despair sit and croak." We shall hear in solemn ecstasy the music from invisible instruments as unseen musicians, knowing the time of God's redemptive purpose through Christ and of God's purpose of grace through Israel, build reeling palaces of

melody before the eyes of our souls. We shall get
glimpses of the outer darkness where no angel of light
chases away its foul vapors, where no rivers roll to cool
its oceans of liquid fire. We shall—no doubt—stumble
and cry out for fear as we hear serpents hissing in every
gorge, as we see hideous goblins dancing on every hill,
as we see specters creep from every rock while phan-
toms ride on every wind and demons sit on every
mountain.

Yes, if we look upon the last week of the public ministry of Jesus on this earth as a continent, we shall see
within that continent the grandeur of all mountains tower-
ing in one snow-capped, cloud-wrapped, sunlit Himalayan
peak. We shall see the force of all rivers in one flood-
tide river. We shall hear the thunderous voice of all
cataracts pouring forth in one Niagara of glory. We
shall see, as those who behold tabernacled suns, the
prophetic sunlight of many centuries bursting forth in a
focus of splendor—and shining in unspeakable glory
within the narrow limits of one swiftly-passing, shadowed
week. And we shall walk with the shadows of all darkness—the darkness of foul caves, the darkness of stormy
nights, the darkness of hell's deep dungeons, the darkness
of men's mad death plots, all about us.

There, within the narrow limits of that week, we shall
see the flowers of a thousand spring-times blossoming in
the narrow limits of one seven-day garden—the roots of
the flowers reaching deep into the past. There, too, we
shall see thorns as the ripened fruit of men's hate—
thorns that puncture and lacerate under the pressure of
men's hands the holy brow upon which "majestic sweetness sits enthroned." There, by prayer, and by the guid-
ance of the Holy Spirit, we shall have some under-

standing of the weight of agony and the pain pressure of sorrows that weighed upon the Savior's heart. There where the sorrows of sin and life and death found utterance in a silent and sometimes weeping Savior, we shall hear the fury of all storms, cyclonic and tornadic and simoonic and hurricanic gathered into one black cloud that bursts with a fury that exceeds the bursting of explosive shells, as the hatreds of men and the furies of hell make mad assault on Jesus—until no power was left in bramble or javelin or thorn or scourge or nail to hurt the dead Son of God. There, exploring the confines and corners of that week, we hear the sob of all the sorrows of sorrow. There we hear the raucous clamor of all snarls. There we see the Christ thrust forth into the fountainless deserts of men's scorn—a desolate Sahara where, for his burning thirst, no water is—where, in the heat of man's despising, no shadow is.

Considering him who *suffered* that week, considering him who *sorrowed* that week, considering him whom we behold *dying* that week—dying with the meekness of "a lamb led to the slaughter and as a sheep dumb before her shearers"—dying with the sublimity of an eagle defying the attacks of twittering sparrows, dying with the sweetness of a saint in prayer, dying with the courage of a martyr who murmurs not in the flames and cries not out on the torture rack,—considering *him*, I say, the events of that week are the values of all diamonds in one lustrous diamond, the glory of all opals in one opal, the eloquence of all eloquence in one utterance, the pathos of all tragedies in one tragedy, the abyss of all depths in one vast abyss of woe, the cruelty of all cruelties in one wild, diabolic orgy of hate and envy.

That last week is a deep still pool. In this pool gold and silver fish dart playfully. That week is also a troubled sea—a sea full of slow-heaving, slimy monsters. That week is a tangled wood, thicker than forest primeval, wherein no man can claim to know all the way. That week is an abyss of woe, a chasm of mystery, a field of wonder, where even the feet of deity drew back from the horrors sin imposed. That week is a house whose windows are darkness and whose walls are confusion, where the shuddering necessity of a world's sins uttered itself at midnight. That week is a shadowy garden, where the roots of Christ's divine emotion put forth their crimson tears, where his soul was "exceedingly sorrowful unto death." That week is a cup wherein Christ and his friends found bitter draughts and dregs—a cup wherein his enemies found zest and rejoicing. That last week is a fountain of hate at which some drank copiously—and returned with bloody hands to drink again. That week is a fountain where some drank "the honeyed depths of Love's sacrifice." That week is an ocean—swept with storms, infested with sharks, and wild with man's butcherous orgies of torment. That week reveals to us the throne of God, reveals the council chamber of devils, reveals the dwelling of angels, reveals the vile heath of witches' Sabbaths, reveals the nursery of sweet children, the blood-spattered scenes of nameless tragedies.

LISTEN! Let your ears, by the Holy Spirit, become keenly sensitized. Within the corridors of that week you hear strange things! Mothers sob. Women wail. Mad men shriek and curse. There are love-croonings. There are cries of agonized terror. There are hymns of love. There is the roaring of lynch mobs. There are the kisses of lovers and the kisses of traitors. Are you listening?

There—the thud of clenched fists beating a face white like a hawthorne blossom. There—the sound of fleeing feet. There—the prayers of agonized souls. There—the curses of mad men. There—the shouts of glad men. There—the drip of blood, "drawn from Immanuel's veins." There, at one and the same time, the bleat of sheep and the snarl of wolves. Do you hear? There, in mysterious contemporaneousness, the rush of angry winds and the whisper of sweet zephyrs. There, in one breath and with many breathings, you smell fumes from the sulphurous pits of hell and fragrance from the crushed Lily of the Valley and the bruised Rose of Sharon fair. There, whether you rest or run, you will feel the warmth of friendly fires and the chill of icy fiendishness. There, as two bugles that blow simultane-ously, you hear the music of sweet old harps by angel fingers touched and the mournful monotony of raucous inharmony produced by Satan's jubilators. There, you will look into eyes that are homes of silent prayer. There you will look into malicious eyes that blaze with hate— their sockets shining as sulphur fires burning in darkened pits. There, as snakes and doves that meet in one cellar, you will hear the hiss of human serpents, the offspring of vipers, and the whispers of lovers at trysting places. There, if you have proper measure of spiritual discern-ment, you will see evil faces on which few traces of virtue are found. You will see, too, faces drawn with agony and washed with tears—tears which reveal the sympathetic agony of faithful hearts.

There, no matter where you go within the confines of that week, no matter into which corners you look, you will hear the flutter of angel's wings and, at the same time and at the same place, the footfalls of demons.

And I want us to give thought to the proximities of that eventful week—the THINGS TWO—which we find. Not the directive TO—showing direction. Not the excessive TOO—signifying excess. But the numerical TWO—giving evidence of proximity, supposed or real.

Surely you will not feel the thorns of roses without smelling the fragrance the roses have and give. Surely, if you walk without vanity, God will be favorable unto you and you will see his face with joy, and no wearisome journeyings will be appointed unto you. Surely, if, with eyes that see, you walk worshipfully amidst these wonders, you will never have cause to say what Madam De Berney said when, at the expense of her own life, she gave liberty to Balzac: "If I could only forget, if I could only forget."

CHAPTER II

THE TWO PROCESSIONS

"Jesus entered into Jerusalem"—MARK 11:11.
*"Pilate . . . delivered Jesus to their will . . . and . . .
they led him away"*—LUKE 23:24-26.

1. *Think of Processions.*

The Bible, in language vivid and strong, speaks of some processions. There is, for example, the procession into Noah's Ark—built as God said, and finished in God's time.

> *"And Noah went in, and his sons, and his wife, and his sons' wives with him, into the ark, because of the waters of the flood. Of clean beasts, and of beasts that are not clean, and of fowls, and of every thing that creepeth upon the earth, there went in two and two unto Noah into the ark, the male and the female, as God had commanded Noah"*—GENESIS 7:7-9.

Think, too, of the procession, when a nation of millions was born in a night, as, by the leadership of Moses, God "brought his people out that he might bring them in" (Deut. 6:23).

> *"And he called for Moses and Aaron by night, and said, Rise up, and get you forth from among my people, both ye and the children of Israel; and go, serve the Lord, as ye have said. Also take your flocks and your herds, as ye have said, and be gone;*
> *"And the people took their dough before it was leavened, their kneadingtroughs being bound up in their clothes upon their shoulders.*

"And the children of Israel journeyed from Rameses to Succoth, about six hundred thousand on foot that were men, beside children. And a mixed multitude went up also with them; and flocks, and herds, even very much cattle"—Exodus 12:31, 32, 34, 37-38..

Consider also the procession when David brought the Ark of the Covenant to Jerusalem—the time when, in spiritual ecstasy, he danced before the Lord:

"And it was told king David, saying, The Lord hath blessed the house of Obededom, and all that pertaineth unto him, because of the ark of God. So David went and brought up the ark of God from the house of Obededom into the city of David with gladness. And it was so, and when they that bare the ark of the Lord had gone six paces, he sacrificed oxen and fatlings. And David danced before the Lord with all his might; and David was girded with a linen ephod. So David and all the house of Israel brought up the ark of the Lord with shouting, and with the sound of the trumpet"
—II Samuel 6:12-15.

Give thought now—a minute or so—to the procession at Solomon's inaugural—after the completion of the glorious Temple in the construction of which one hundred and eighty-three thousand, six hundred men worked seven and one-half years.

"Thus all the work that Solomon made for the house of the Lord was finished: and Solomon brought all the things in that David his father had dedicated; and the silver, and the gold, and all the instruments, put he among the treasures of the house of God. Then Solomon assembled the elders of Israel, and all the heads of the tribes, the chief of the fathers of the children of Israel, unto Jerusalem, to bring up the ark of the covenant of the Lord out of the city of David, which is Zion.

Wherefore all the men of Israel assembled themselves unto the king in the feast which was in the seventh month. And all the elders of Israel came; and the Levites took up the ark. And they brought up the ark, and the tabernacle of the congregation, and all the holy vessels that were in the tabernacle, these did the priests and the Levites bring up. Also king Solomon, and all the congregation of Israel that were assembled unto him before the ark, sacrificed sheep and oxen, which could not be told nor numbered for multitude"
II Chron. 5:1-6.

And remember that you can not call that any small procession in which you find the Queen of Sheba coming to visit Solomon:

"And when the queen of Sheba heard of the fame of Solomon, she came to prove Solomon with hard questions at Jerusalem, with a very great company, and camels that bare spices, and gold in abundance, and precious stones: and when she was come to Solomon, she communed with him of all that was in her heart"
—II Chron. 9:1.

And certainly we would not say that the triumphal processions of Caesar should not be noted—the great celebrations by which military heroes in the days of the Roman commonwealth signalized their victories on their return to the city. As we have read, "in these triumphal processions, everything was set forth in exhibition which could serve as a symbol of the conquered country or a trophy of victory." "Flags and banners taken from the enemy; vessels of gold and silver, and other treasures, loaded in vans; wretched captives conveyed in open carriages or marching sorrowfully on foot, and destined, some of them, to public execution when the ceremony of the triumph was ended; displays of arms, and implements and dresses, and all else which might serve to give the Roman crowd an idea of the customs and usages of the remote and conquered nations; the animals they used, caparisoned in the manner in which they used them. These and a thousand other trophies and emblems were brought into the line to excite the admiration of the crowd, and to add to the gorgeousness of the spectacle. Once, in these triumphs of Caesar, a young sister of Cleopatra was in the line of the Egyptian procession. In that devoted to Asia Minor was a great banner containing the words already referred to, VENI, VIDI, VICI. There were great paintings, too, borne aloft, representing battles and other striking scenes. Of course, all Rome was in the highest state of excitement during the days of the exhibition of this pageantry. The whole surrounding country flocked to the capital to witness it, and Caesar's greatness and glory were signalized in the most conspicuous manner to all mankind."

I am sure that all of us, at one time or another, have been interested in the descriptions that have been given of what is known as "The John Howard Payne Procession." We have been told how, this great American went over to Africa, died, and was buried—and slept in his grave until 1883. Then there came a day when his remains were dug up and put in a metallic casket. We are told how the United States Government sent a man-of-war and, with the coffin draped in the American flag, with the Stars and Stripes flying at half mast, that battleship started out through the Mediterranean, passed through the Strait of Gibraltar, and across the Atlantic, entered the harbor of New York—and, as the ship entered the harbor, guns thundered the salute of honor. Flags of all nations, of all ships, dipped their colors and all the forts thundered a welcome. They put that coffin aboard a special train. From Jersey City, on the Pennsylvania, they hurried it to Washington. Business was suspended. The house of representatives and the Senate closed. All department stores, schools, and universities suspended. There, as we have been told, on the reviewing stand stood the President, members of his cabinet! Here, the United States Supreme Court! Here, officers of the army! Here, officers of the navy! Here, heads of the departments! Here, senators, representatives! And the population stood with bowed, uncovered heads while the streets were lined with school children, each with an American flag turned upside down in honor, as down Pennsylvania Avenue, went the procession headed by the Marine band.

I would ask you, too, to compare the great procession at the Queen's Jubilee in June, 1897, and the still more magnificent Durbar at Delhi, India, in 1912, in honor of King George V. No Roman triumph was ever so magnificent, or meant a millionth part as much for good. The whole empire was enthused. Princes of India and premiers of the eleven self-governed colonies, with their suites and soldiers, brought brilliancy to the show, and demonstrated the extent of the military resources of the empire.

Now step back across the centuries and think of how Herodotus records that when Xerxes was passing over the bridge of the Hellespont, the way before him was strewed with branches of myrtle, while burning perfumes filled the air. Quintius Curtius tells of the scattering of flowers in the way before Alexander, the Great, when he entered Babylon.

Think of Pompey's triumph in September, B.C., 61. About ninety years before Christ's triumphal entry, the most magnificent triumph ever seen in Rome was given to Pompey. For two days the grand procession of trophies from every land and a long retinue of captives moved into the city along the Via Sacra. Brazen tablets were carried on which were engraved the names of the conquered nations, including one thousand castles and nine hundred cities. The remarkable circumstance of the celebration was that it declared him conqueror of the whole world.

Think again of how Julius Caesar entered Rome in a car drawn by forty elephants, of how Mark Anthony entered the city in a chariot to which lions were harnessed, of how Aurelian was conveyed to the Capitol in a gilded chariot drawn by four stags, of how, even in our day, Monier saw the way of a Persian ruler strewn with roses for three miles while glass vessels filled with sugar were broken under his horses' feet—the sugar being symbolical of prosperity.

You might think also of Xerxes passing over the bridge of the Hellespont—the way before him strewed with myrtle branches while perfumes filled the air.

2. *See Jesus Enter Jerusalem.*

Of all the processions, mentioned and unmentioned, publicized and unpublicized, there has been no procession like that when Jesus, himself the living ark of the world's salvation, entered Jerusalem in royal state—that only hour of royal pomp he ever had on earth, that hour speaking as eloquently of his humiliation as the long reaches of his lowly life. For this procession was eloquent of the earthly poverty of him who, while foxes had holes and birds had nests, had nowhere to lay his head, had no pocket-book save the mouth of a fish. A Prince that day, all his true followers weaponless and powerless, he was a pauper prince on a borrowed ass— the commonest beast for everybody to ride, making the pauper Prince as not above the people in his manner and ordering of earthly state.

Possessing the true kingly spirit—a spirit, not of pride, but of lowliness—a spirit, not of exultation, but of daily service and helpfulness, sanctifying and exalting common things—a spirit, not afar off in seclusion, but near the people—not receiving *from* the people, but giving *to* them, full of compassion, the King of Love rides.

And all this was in accordance with Jesus' plan of a spiritual kingdom—a kingdom of truth, of righteousness, of peace, of brotherhood, of love. There was no herald, no standard of revolt, nothing to excite the antagonisms of the Romans. As someone has wisely told us, the Jews in Jerusalem, many of them, had seen Jewish military heroes return in triumph from successful wars. Some were still living who could remember Herod the Great, riding at the head of an army to defy the haughty Sanhedrin that had summoned him to trial. Some had seen Cassius, the gray-headed triumvir, arriving with his Roman cohorts. Some had seen the swift-moving Parthians sweeping with victorious insolence over Palestine to seat Antigonus on the throne. Some had seen Herod, backed by the might and glory of Rome, leading Mariame as his bride, entering the ancient capitol of Judea to seat himself in splendor on the blood-stained throne in the city of King David. But of all who saw Jesus enter Jerusalem, who could see any militarily ordered array? Who could see soldierly-disciplined ranks armed to the teeth? Who could see glittering steel thrust out? Or gleam of brass helmet or copper shield? Or Roman short sword thirsty for blood? Or long Thracian spike keen to kill? Or neighing and prancing war horses? Or rolling war chariot with knives of death on wheel rims?

Jesus, leaving Bethpage, rode toward Jerusalem, the royal city, the city of the Great King, where his ancester David reigned. The "most part of a great multitude" (for there were some cold and scowling critics—Luke 19:39-40) — pilgrims, numbering nearly three million souls, from all parts of the country coming up to the Passover festival—spread their garments in the way as a recognized act of homage to a King. Some took off their outer robes—somewhat on the principle that— centuries later—actuated the heart of young Sir Walter Raleigh, when, on Queen Elizabeth coming to a miry part of the road, and hesitating for an instant how to step across, he "took off his new plush mantle and spread it on the ground."

"Others cut down branches." The imperfect tense here denotes continued action—they kept on cutting branches and spreading them. Dr. Vincent in "Word Studies" says: "Matthew, Mark, and John use each a different word for *branches*. Matthew, a word meaning a young slip, or shoot; a twig as related to a branch. Mark, a word meaning a litter of branches and leaves cut from the fields near by; a mass of straw, rushes, or leaves beaten together, or strewed loose, so as to form a bed or a carpeted way. John, strictly palm branches, the feathery fronds forming the tufted crown of the tree."

"The multitudes that went before and followed." Stanley makes this comment: "Two vast streams of people met on that day. The one poured out from the city; and, as they came through the gardens whose clusters of palm rose on the southeastern corner of Olivet, they cut down the long branches, and moved toward Bethany with shouts of welcome. From Bethany streamed forth the crowds who had assembled there the previous night. The two streams met midway. Half of the vast mass, turning round, preceded; the other half followed." Now that great multitude that accompanied Jesus filled the Pharisees with malice and envy—because every method they had taken to hinder the people from following Jesus had proved ineffectual.

> *"The Pharisees therefore said among themselves, Perceive ye how ye prevail nothing? behold, the world is gone after him"*—JOHN 12:19.

"Cried, saying, Hosanna." "Hosanna," we learn, is a rendering into Greek letters of the Hebrew words, "Save, we pray" (Psalm 118:25). It is like a shout of "Salvation, salvation!" It is used as an expression of praise, like "Hallelujah" or "Hail". It was a kind of *holy hurrah*. Had the event occurred in Rome, the shout would have been *Io Triumphe!* Had it occurred in modern France, the people would have called out *Vive*. It is thus remarkably like the aspiration or petition that is breathed in England's national anthem, "God Save the Queen!"

"Hosanna!"—"Blessed is he that cometh in the name of the Lord!" "Hosanna in the highest"—in the highest degree, in the highest strains, in the highest heavens. "Hosanna to the son of David!" "Blessed is he!" "Blessed is the King!" "Blessed is the King of Israel that cometh in the name of the Lord!" "Blessed be the Kingdom of our father David that cometh in the name of the Lord!" "Peace in heaven and glory in the highest!" Putting together all the records, we see how manifold were the shouts of triumph. These shouted expressions were taken mostly from the 118th Psalm—the Messianic Psalm—which Chadwick calls "that great song of triumph, which told how the nations, swarming like bees, were quenched like the light fire of thorns, how the right hand of the Lord did valiantly, how the gates of righteousness should be thrown open for the righteous, and, more significant still, how the stone which the builders rejected should become the headstone of the corner."

This great throng came into Jerusalem. And who was in that supreme cavalcade of the world? Amos Wells, servant of God, asks us to think about those who may have been in that procession—when, for Jesus, it was roses and palm branches and garments and hosannas all the way—as Jesus was the central figure of that procession into the city.

Recalling some rich remarks of Dr. Amos Wells, I say that I love to think that the man whose withered hand was made whole was there—happily plucking and throwing more palm branches than anyone else. I love to think that some of the lepers Jesus had healed were there—glad that they could mingle with people once more, never again having to dwell apart shunned by all mankind, never again uttering or hearing, as those who hear the sentence of death, the horrible old cry, "Unclean! Unclean!" I love to think that deaf people whom Jesus had cured were there—their restored ear drums keenly sensitized to every whispering wind, to every singing bird, to every voice of that momentous day. I love to think that the Gadarene demoniac whose deranged reason

Jesus had restored and whose self-inflicted wounds Jesus had cured, was there—not raving and foaming now, not naked now, but "eager to take off his coat and fling it down before his Savior." I love to think that the man who was laid at the Pool of Bethesda so long and who passed thirty-eight years away never making a step, was there—not impotent now but running and leaping as the hart, even as sin-crippled men saved by Jesus have been running ever since. I love to think that Bartimaeus was there — no longer blind, no longer begging, but his sparkling eyes taking in all the glories of field and forest, earth and sky, stream and hill. I love to think that dumb people whom Jesus had healed were there—singing in their hearts that they could shout, singing with their lips the praises of Jesus, the Light of the world. I love to think the woman whom Jesus met at Sychar was there—remembering the day she met him at Jacob's well and cherishing in her heart the things he had said unto her. I love to think that the owner of the colt on which Jesus rode was there—glad, as all have been glad ever since, that he had the smallest share in one of Christ's triumphs. I love to think that his mother was there—her heart full of things the tongue can not utter—and Mary, out of whom he had cast seven devils, once devil-possessed, now devotion-possessed. I love to think the woman who touched his garment's hem was there, and the widow of Nain—and other women whom Jesus had helped and blessed.

And I can see also a great host out of all ages past, looking eagerly on. Was not John the Baptist there? Were not Moses and Elijah? And David and Samuel? And Abraham and Jacob? And Daniel and Isaiah? I think of these as watching all of Christ's triumphs ever since. I believe that in all triumphal processions there are invisible people accompanying the visible throng. There is certainly the "choir invisible" — sometimes chanting dirges over the wrecks, the distress and poverty and bloodshed, ravaged fields, ruined villages, widows and orphans, crimes and cruelties, which the victories left in their path—some time singing hymns of joy over the good accomplished, the progress of all that is good for mankind, intermingled with many a minor chord of sorrow. If Christ had opened the eyes of these looking upon this scene as the eyes of Elisha's servant were opened at Dothan, so that they might see the invisible and hear the inaudible, no pen could picture all who march in the real triumphal procession. They adorn the highways of the centuries. Joining this throng are multitudes delivered from the bondage of their sins—and brought into the light of the Gospel. Joining this throng the angels who sang at his birth, Moses and Elijah who appeared on the Mount of Transfiguration, John the Baptist who baptized Jesus, the twelve legions of angels he once said were ready at his call, the heavenly choirs who sing their songs of joy over many sinners brought to repentance. Oh, what a procession was this with its visible and invisible hosts! Not all of earth's monarchs could have summoned such a procession. In the procession on the earth—a great multitude. In the air around and above the actual procession a great multitude—as the space around Raphael's picture of the infant Jesus is filled with a cloud of angel faces. And the procession has not stopped. All the redeemed, ten thousand times ten thousand and thousands of thousands, are singing his hosannas and joining in the song:

*"Saying with a loud voice, Worthy is the Lamb that
was slain to receive power, and riches, and wisdom,
and strength, and honour, and glory, and blessing.
And every creature which is in heaven, and on the
earth, and such as are in the sea, and all that are in
them, heard I saying, Blessing, and honour, and glory,
and power, be unto him that sitteth upon the throne,
and unto the Lamb forever and ever"*—REV. 5:12-13.

3. *See Jesus Go Out from Jerusalem.*

So near in point of time—these two processions. So
far apart as to the treatment of Jesus—the central figure
of both processions. Coming *into* the city "the whole
enthusiasm of the multitude at the end is nothing more
than the last upstreaming of an evening sun before it
vanishes beneath the horizon." For Jesus was riding to
his death, though many knew it not. Just a few days
after that day of triumph, they brought him out *from*
the city—him who was scourge-cut, and thorn-crowned
and bruised and beaten—leading him to Golgotha, the
place of a skull. And history contains no parallel to this
extraordinary spectacle. Napoleon Bonaparte on the
deck of the British "Bellerophon" going into exile on the
inhospitable island of St. Helena, was a defeated conqueror. Louis XVI, going through the streets of Paris
on the way to the guillotine, and Charles I, in front of
his palace at Whitehall, placing his head on the block,
were paying the penalty of extreme selfishness and misdoing. But Christ, loved of God and hated of men, gave
himself for the people—the Just One for the unjust, the
innocent for the guilty.

How soon the popular demonstration had given way
to the popular denunciation! The day of triumph was
so closely followed by a day of tragedy. The day of
crucifixion so close on the heels of the day of palms—a

midnight so near a sunburst in a clear mid-heaven. And how different that procession moving *out of the city* from that procession going *into the city.* Pilate, having yielded to the clamors of the Jews, delivered Jesus up to death. And Jesus was led away to be crucified—to the place called Calvary, "an isolated white limestone knoll, in contour like the crown of the head, and about sixty feet high."

"Under that festal sky through that festal crowd," slow as a funeral crowd, that procession first moved westward through the Via Dolorosa, to the road leading northward to the Damascus gate. Passing through the gate, it turned eastward along the north wall of the city, winding north and west over the eastern end of Calvary till they reached the western and highest summit. In advance was a soldier carrying a white wooden board on which was written the nature of the crime. Next came four soldiers, under a centurion, with the hammer and the nails, guarding Jesus, who bore, as always in such cases, the cross on which he was to suffer.

> *"And he bearing his cross went forth into a place called the place of a skull, which is called in the Hebrew, Golgotha"*—JOHN 19:17.

Then came two robbers, each bearing his cross, and guarded by four soldiers. As they went forth into the street, they were followed by a great multitude—many with eager curiosity, priests exulting over their enemy. The scene is vividly described in "Ben Hur": "He was nearly dead. Every few steps he staggered as if he would fall. A stained gown, badly torn, hung from his shoulders over a seamless under tunic. An inscription on a board was tied to his neck. A crown of thorns had been

crushed hard down upon his head. . . . The mob sometimes broke through the guard and struck him with sticks
and spit upon him. Yet no sound escaped him, neither
remonstrance nor groan."

So soon it was that Jesus, weak and weary from his
long vigils and sufferings, was unable to bear the weight
of the cross. The fatigue of the preceding night, spent
without sleep, the sufferings he had undergone in the
Garden of Gethsemane, where the roots of his divine
emotion put forth their crimson tears, his having been
hurried from place to place—obliged to stand the whole
time of his trials, the want of food, the loss of blood he
had sustained, and not his want of courage on this occasion, made him faint under the burden of his cross.

The crown of thorns was still on his head, his face was
toward the dirty street. His eyes, deep sunk in their
sockets, burned as weak lamps that struggle to keep
aglow in a tempest. He was bowed down almost to
the ground by the cross which was laid on his back,
tying his arms around it backward. And, as Asch says,
that cross was heavy with more than its own weight—
and that invisible burden pressed his body down, so that
it would break at any moment. He strove forward, thus
oppressed, and every step came slowly, with infinite pain
—"like the splitting of the Red Sea"—his legs and arms
quivering under the load and the lash. "His footsteps
left red imprints on the stones." Jesus gasps for breath.
One knee yielded under him slowly, with pain. "And the
cross, with all the invisible burden which lay upon it,
collapsed on him." The soldiers, seeing him unable to
bear the weight of the cross, laid it on one Simon, a
native of Cyrene, in Northern Africa, the father of
Alexander and Rufus, well known later among the first

Christians, and forced him to bear it. The soldiers goadingly drove Simon as though he were an ox instead of a man. And Jesus, every breath He drew a pang of pain, every movement of every muscle a torture, followed painfully after Simon—carrying the cross to Golgotha, and to God's hall of eternal fame. And Jesus as he followed was still bowed earthward, "as if only the cross had been lifted from him, but not the invisible burden." The soldiers did not, however, make Simon do this out of compassion to the suffering Jesus, but to prevent his dying with the painful fatigue—and by that means eluding his punishment. Anyway, on to Golgotha goes Simon. And on to Golgotha goes Jesus. And on to Golgotha go the soldiers of Rome. And on to its bloody scenes the lamenting women. And—some men, too. And you and I, because of our sins, were there taking part in that crucifixion torture.

But we are not yet through with these scenes—as you will understand when you hear the message on the two weepings of that last week of Jesus' public ministry.

Chapter III

THE TWO WEEPINGS

"He beheld the city and wept over it"—Luke 19:41.
"A great company of people and of women ... bewailed and lamented him"—Luke 23:27.

We take these two weepings in reverse order—because of what we have just been thinking as to the procession to Calvary.

The blessed Jesus, in his painful journey to Calvary, was followed by an innumerable multitude of people, particularly of women, who lamented bitterly the severity of his sentence, and showed all tokens of sincere compassion and grief. And the grief of these women was keener than the grief of "a stranger-tended child, which seeks its mother's arms, and sees and feels them not." And you could not describe that grief by saying that "woman's grief is like a summer storm, short as it is violent." No. Nothing like that—nothing like a shallow stream of sympathy that ran under strain a fuller course.

But Luke gives us the touching story of the women of Jerusalem expressing their sympathetic grief in tears. The women, their hearts full of misery, through compassionate eyes filled with tears, saw his face swollen with bruises, dirty with the sputum of foul mouths from which he had not hidden his face—and they wept. The women saw some clenched fists raised above the heads of others and shaken at Jesus—and the women wept. They saw the tormented Nazarene among those so blind to the beauty of his character, among those so unresponsive to the magnanimity of his nature—and the women wept.

They saw Jesus under his cross, saw him dragging it along with the invisible burden that lay a-top of it—and the women wept. The women saw him bowed earthward —struggling as an exhausted swimmer among the debris of strong currents of a treacherous river—and the women wept. The women saw his blood-stained robe shining among the spears of the soldiers—and the women wept. They saw his cloak and shirt soaked through and through with blood and sweat—and the women wept. They saw him reel and stagger beneath the cross—lying there like a wounded lamb beneath the hoof and tusks of a wild boar—and the women wept. Yes, women who weep over broken bird's nests, who weep when others weep, who weep over the hurts of their children, who weep when they separate from loved ones, who cry in travail— "bewailed and lamented him." And their tears were the first and only drops that fell like refreshing showers in the hot sands of his burning and shadeless desert that day. These women, bewailing and lamenting him, saw the drops of blood congealed on his face, and wrung their hands—weeping. Then Jesus, who always felt the woes of others more than he did his own, forgetting his distress at the very time when it lay heaviest upon him, turned himself about, and, with a benevolence and tenderness truly divine, said to them:

> *"Daughters of Jerusalem, weep not for me, but weep for yourselves, and for your children. For, behold, the days are coming, in the which they shall say, Blessed are the barren, and the wombs that never bare, and the paps which never gave suck. Then shall they begin to say to the mountains, Fall on us; and to the hills, Cover us. For if they do these things in a green tree, what shall be done in the dry?"*—LUKE 23:28-31.

Forgetting his own sufferings, Jesus, "made of a woman, made under the law to redeem them that were under the law, that we might receive the adoption of sons" (Gal 4:4), appealed to them to use their influence to avert the terrible doom of the city, which was to fall so heavily on the women and children. As if he said, Dry up those tears, ye daughters of Jerusalem, which ye shed in compassion to me, and reserve them for the deplorable fate of yourselves, and of your children; for the calamities that will soon fall on you and your offspring are truly terrible, and call for the bitterest lamentations. In those days of vengeance, you will passionately wish that you had not given birth to a generation whose wickedness had rendered them the objects of the wrath of the Almighty, to such a degree as never was before experienced in the world. Then they shall wish to be crushed under the weight of enormous mountains, and concealed from their enemies in the bowels of the hills. The thoughts of these calamities afflict my soul far more than the feelings of my own sufferings. For if the Jews and Romans are permitted to inflict such punishments on me, who am innocent, how dreadful must the vengeance be which they shall inflict on a nation whose sins cry aloud to heaven, hastening the pace of the divine judgments, and rendering the perpetrators as proper for punishment as dry wood is for the flames.

But of the weeping of the women would I not have you think, further, just now. I would have you think now of that other weeping—so near in point of time, yet far, in cause, apart—the weeping of Jesus. And certainly we know that His tears were not "tears of joy, like summer raindrops, pierced by sunbeams"—not tears that heralded smiles "like April does the sunny May"—not "funeral tears that from different causes rise"—not tears like the "iron tears flowing down Pluto's cheeks," but tears superiorly akin to "holy tears in heavenly eyes that speak of woe succeeding woe, as wave a wave." From his eyes "a stream of tears descended like a broken necklace of pearls." His tears "shone as the dew on a lily, at the rising of the sun." "Fresh tears stood on his cheeks as doth the honey dew upon a gathered lily almost withered."

> *"And when he was come near, he beheld the city, and wept over it"*—LUKE 19:41.

Yes—"he beheld the city and wept over it"—notwithstanding the many affronts he had received there.

"He beheld the city."

And, oh, what a sight for the eyes to which midnight was as the noonday. There was Jerusalem—glorious, guilty, queenly Jerusalem—the dream city of the Jews, the city of God, the center of one thousand years of national memories, the city toward which prophets, with outstretched hands and eyes that burned with a strange light, prayed. There was Jerusalem whose past shone gloriously as the full moon shining on midnight seas, but in whose sacred courts evil was girt with diadem. There was Jerusalem! For Jerusalem kings had kneeled down and prayed. For her prophets had wept. For Jerusalem martyrs had burned to sizzling cinders in the fire. Jerusalem, which had a virgin's eyes, though having been warmed by the suns and chilled by the winters of a thousand years. Jerusalem—in whose eyes lay—deep folded—prophecies of him who had glory with God before the world was. Jerusalem—with evil heart and bloody hands—having played the harlot with many strange lovers.

Yes, "he beheld the city"—its long line of white city walls lying like snow barricades. The glorious panorama of the city burst upon his sight quickly from the Mount of Olives—as a flower, sun-warmed and wind-kissed, bursts into bloom. Towers of alabaster and domes of gilt gleamed "like flocks of cloudlets bright in sunny air at noon," "like the galleons rare of an argonaut's dream," "like spring's white bloom on boughs all gaunt and gnarry," "as the brows of the billows that brighten the storm with their crests," like star beams of "some high predominant star." There the palace of Caiaphas and David's tomb "gleamed as funeral lamps in an open sepulcher." The grand colonnade of Herod's home gleaming with white marble, reaching a height of two hundred feet, shone "like a patch of moon on mountain peak." Silvery Siloam, underneath jutting rocks, gleams "like a bride at her looking glass."

There was the whole panorama of Jerusalem—the Antonia fortress, whence, on many occasions, the Roman military governor "lay on his couch under his parasol and gazed down contemptuously at the rites performed in the Temple." Jesus saw this fortress like a frowning face amid happier faces. He saw the pretentious suburban homes of the wealthy Jews and "the mud huts of the lower city, the hidden heaps of the valley of Kidron —the camping ground of the outcast lepers."

Sholem Asch* describes it for us in weighty and beautiful words: "Jerusalem has been likened to a hart which leaps from mountain top to mountain top. Its houses, its palaces, towers, citadels and walls were lifted on heights and lowered into valleys. The sight was most glorious, for it was the first hour of noon; the heavens, illumined by the fresh spring sun, were unfolded

* By permission of G. P. Putnam Sons, Publishers, New York.

above the innumerable buildings like the wings of a hen above her chicks. And one would have said that the city was built not of clay and stone, but of silver. On many of the roofs there were water cisterns; and those that were below the level of our eyes flung back the sunlight at us; they were like precious jewels in the walls which girdled Jerusalem. Yet the city had broken through the girdle; it poured out toward Mount Scopus; it stretched toward Bethlem and reached out to Bet Paga. Out of the walls rose, like mighty breasts, the towers and watch turrets, with those of the Herodian palace dominating the rest. And all the city, houses, towers and walls, was spread like a conquered army at the foot of the flaming Mount of the House. The Temple, with its golden gates and balconies, was like an uplifted flame. From our place toward the foot of the Mount of Olives it seemed like something which no human hand had reared out of earthly substance; it was like a vision which had descended, perfect and glorious, from the heavens; flaming walls, flaming gates, flaming roofs. From the heart of the golden House rose a pillar of smoke. Below it was yellow flame, and above it was transparent gray cloud, which broke into floating rings. The appearance of the Temple was unearthly, strange, unbelievable. Only behind the vision of the Temple there rose a gray stone citadel, lofty, insolent, like a threatening spear held by a mighty fist."

"Eklausen!" "Jesus wept." He wailed aloud, the tears streaming down his face. What wretchedness—in that city. What wickedness! What future calamities awaited Jerusalem! Knowing the end from the beginning, his tender heart revealed itself through eyes that ran tears. No wonder. Wherever he looked he found unhappiness.

Discontented and bitter the upper classes. **Sullen and
hopeless the lower classes!** Insecure was life. Insecure
was property. The city with alarming rumors, jealousies,
suspicion and fierce debates was filled. There poverty
added horror to horror. He saw Jerusalem as she was—
in her sorrow. The vision of that city's sin and doom
rising from the gates and domes and palaces, obliterated
the landscape from horizon to horizon, and he burst into
tears. He saw the city adorned as a bride, but her bride-
groom was riding to his death. So—"he wept over the
city."

Yes, Jesus wept—lifted up his voice in tearful, painful
wailing. And said:

> *"If thou hadst known, even thou, at least in this thy
> day, the things which belong unto thy peace! but now
> they are hid from thine eyes. For the days shall come
> upon thee, that thine enemies shall cast a trench about
> thee, and compass thee round, and keep thee in on
> every side, and shall lay thee even with the ground,
> and thy children within thee; and they shall not leave
> in thee one stone upon another; because thou knewest
> not the time of thy visitation"*—LUKE 19:42-44.

And that—although all the agonies and insults a few
days later could not wring from him one sigh or tear.
Jesus did never weep for himself. The merciless scourge
of Pilate that seamed his quivering flesh until it started
up in red scars did not make him cry for himself. The
cruel fingers that plucked out his beard and the thorns
that punctured his brow could not make him cry for himself. The nails that nailed him to the tree could not
make him weep for pain's sake. But the tears he shed
over Jerusalem the day he entered the city were the
prelusive drops of a hurricanic storm that, forty years

later, destroyed the queenliest of all queenly cities. They
went before the great black drops which fell with the
fierceness of hailstones driven by cyclonic winds on the
hot streets—later. Being omniscient—knowing the end
from the beginning—Jesus saw, while the hosannic
shouts of ten thousand throats were "striking column
and pilaster and pillar and wall of cedar and of silver
and of gold, was flung back in numberless echoes," what
some men in that crowd saw forty years later when, in
A.D. 70, Titus sacked the city and demolished its
splendors.

Jesus saw the landscape covered with Roman encamp-
ments. The beautiful city a shapeless ruin with the vul-
tures blackening the sky as they hovered over countless
crosses to feast on the festering bodies of crucified Jews
—the country desolate. Israel wiped out forever. The
temple burned and laid in ruins by the Roman army
under Titus, after the most terrible siege in which the
besieged fought for miserable scraps, chewed belts and
shoes, tore off the leather from their shields and ate
wisps of hay, died by thousands from the horrors of
famine. This siege took place when three million Jews
were crowded into Jerusalem. The siege began at Passover time. Hungry skeletons of the starving walked the
streets. The ground around the city was planted thick
with crosses on which Jews were crucified until there
was not enough soil to hold the crosses and not enough
trees in the woods to make crosses. The doom Christ
foresaw and wept over was fulfilled in throes of agony
more terrible than any known in history.

In these two weepings, we see and hear the weeping
of the women—showing forth the compassion of human
hearts on the miseries of the incarnate Christ. We see

the weeping Savior—setting forth the agony of God's heart over a city that spurned the things that belonged to her peace and salvation.

But who weeps now over our cities? Over London and Chicago and Berlin and Rome and San Francisco? Who weeps now over the fact that there are evils that would lead our greatest graces to the grave and leave the world no copy? Who weeps now over theological prodigals who have left the Father's home of "the faith once for all delivered to the saints" and have gone into the far country? Who weeps now over those who have thrown the Bible into discard—and summon the Bible to appear at the bar of human reason, substituting a "Thus saith the mind of man" for a "Thus saith the Lord"? Who weeps now over girls walking on the edge of an abyss—talking nonsense the while? Who weeps now over the domestic skeletons that cover our land— giving testimony that many orange blossoms have turned to lemon peelings and that much matrimonial milk has been changed to clabber? Who weeps now over men and women who would—judging a tree by its fruit—hand down our blood-bequeathed legacies reduced in quality and in quantity? Who weeps now over young people who cheat themselves with the sound while they spurn the substance? Who weeps now over children, who, because of their godless parents, are more damned into the world than born into it? Who weeps now over those who consider one hour of pleasure today worth one dozen hours of possible safety for tomorrow? Who weeps now over the multitudes misled and unled, who reject the Savior who approaches them with medicine to heal wounds, with pity and power to forgive sins, with love to redeem the life? Who weeps now over those who, on wild seas with their fogs and tempests and treacherous shoals, refuse to set their moral timepiece by the divine Sun? Who weeps now—showing the Christ-like spirit— over those who have well-fed bodies and starved souls— dead souls that have lost their ideals, have given up their dreams and spiritual reveries, their secret prayers, their hidden hopes? Who weeps now, as Christ wept over Jerusalem, over those who nurture not the hours big with character and destiny? *Answer. You* answer. You answer *now.*

> *"Did Christ o'er sinners weep,*
> *And shall our cheeks be dry?*
> *Let floods of penitential grief*
> *Burst forth from every eye."*

How can we, looking upon the weeping Savior, be careless and callous and unconcerned? How *can* we do less than to rejoice that, in love and compassion, Jesus wept? May we be glad to say:

"Jesus wept! those tears are over
        But His heart is still the same,
Kinsman, Friend and Elder Brother,
        Is His everlasting name.
Savior, who can love like Thee,
        Gracious One of Bethany.

"When the pangs of trial seize us,
        When the waves of sorrow roll,
I will lay my head on Jesus,
        Pillow of the troubled soul.
Surely, none can feel like Thee,
        Weeping One of Bethany.

"Jesus wept! and still in glory
        He can mark each mourner's tears;
Living to retrace the story
        Of hearts He solaced here:
Lord, when I am called to die,
        Let me think of Bethany.

"Jesus wept! those tears of sorrow
        As a legacy of love;
Yesterday, today, tomorrow,
        He the same doth ever prove,
Thou art all in all to me,
        Living One of Bethany."

CHAPTER IV

THE TWO THIEVES

"And with him they crucify two thieves; the one on his right hand, and the other on his left. And the scripture was fulfilled, which saith, And he was numbered with the transgressors"—MARK 15:27-28.

What Mark says by the Holy Spirit, Luke also says— by the Spirit.

"And there were also two other malefactors, led with him to be put to death. And when they were come to the place, which is callel Calvary, there they crucified him, and the malefactors, one on the right hand, and the other on the left"—LUKE 23:32-33.

So also John:

"And he bearing his cross went forth into a place called the place of the skull, which is called in the Hebrew, Golgotha: where they crucified him, and two other with him, on either side one, and Jesus in the midst"
—JOHN 19:17-18.

Matthew, too, declares the same truth—

"Then were there two thieves crucified with him, one on the right hand, and another on the left"
—MATT. 27:38.

Call the two who were crucified with him *robbers*. Or call them *thieves*. Both are *malefactors*. Some travelers, no doubt, could testify that by these they had been robbed on the highways of the land. Some home owners, too, could say that by these their houses had been ransacked. Some could assuredly say that by these their lives had been threatened. Many dark nights, with multitudinous tongues, "like the whispering leaves of a wind-stirred oak," could speak of their burglaries. Many bypaths, had they but tongues to talk, could have testified of their dastardly depredations. And these two malefactors, their minds once active in planning crimes, their hearts black with evil, their hands stained with human blood, were crucified with Jesus—to put the same brand upon Jesus. Maybe they—these two evil men— were Jewish fanatics who made insurrection against the Roman power, and used this as a pretext for repine and murder. And with these malefactors, with the intention to give the people an impression that Jesus was to be classed with them, and probably with the purpose to take away the imputation of having punished an innocent man, Jesus was crucified. And thus was fulfilled the prophecy of Isaiah, which reads now, since the crucifixion, more like history than prophecy:

> *"Therefore will I divide him a portion with the great, and he shall divide the spoil with the strong; because he hath poured out his soul unto death: and he was numbered with the transgressors; and he bare the sin of many, and made intercession for the transgressors"*
> —Isa. 53:12.

> *"And the scripture was fulfilled, which saith, And he was numbered with the transgressors"*—Mark 15:28.

And today we who know and believe that Christ, loved by God before the foundation of the world, was "numbered with the transgressors" on Calvary's dark and bloody hill where, "noisy as burial howlers at full cry," "the people . . . and the rulers also with them derided him"—scoffed at him—an unruly, turbulent, shouting, scoffing, mocking crowd, as void of pity as "a maniac drummer in mid battle," a crowd bellowing as does the sea in a tempest, shrieking "like laughter in the demoned hills." And some "fierce as Frenzy's furious blood," said: "He saved others! Let him save himself!" This, of course, he could do if he were Christ, the Messiah. They implied that Christ was a cheat, a mere trickster, who had deceived the people—unless he proved his power by using it to save himself from crucifixion. But he did not come down from the cross. He remained there, while every breath he drew was a torture, while every beat of his heart was cruel pain, in order that he might save others. They imagined that if Christ would do as they proposed they would believe on him:

"He saved others; himself he can not save. If he be the King of Israel, let him now come down from the cross, and we will believe him"—MATT. 27:42.

But they would not have believed. They would have found some other excuse for not believing. For he did something more wonderful than they now asked. He rose from the grave. Yet they did not believe.

And shall we be ashamed of Jesus because he was "numbered with the transgressors"? Shall we blush to own his name because he who numbereth the stars and calleth them by name refused to leave his cross between two thieves? Shall we refuse or fail to give allegiance to him who "bore our sins in his own body on the tree" and became for us—on the cross—all that God must judge that we through faith in him might become all that God cannot judge? God forbid. Listen lovingly to Lorimer: "The Roman would not deny his allegiance to the imperial eagle which he defended, and in our day it would be regarded as baseness for a man to repudiate the mother who bore him, the country that sheltered him, or the college that educated him." Much more base is it for a soul to reject Jesus as Savior, as Prophet, as Priest, as King, and as Lord, in whom is "a glory greater than ever circled the ancient seven-hilled city,"—from whom all of us have received favors which excel in grandeur all that parents, all that country, all that schools can confer. How we label ourselves as cheap and sordid and sinful when, and if, we are ashamed of Jesus.

> *"Ashamed of Jesus! Sooner far*
> *May evening blush to own a star.*
> *Ashamed of Jesus! Just as soon*
> *Might midnight blush to think of noon.*
> *'Twas midnight with my soul till he,*
> *Bright Morning Star, bade darkness flee."*

"Two thieves"—who had cast away in Folly's court and Carnal Pleasure's mart, the wealth God gave them at the start, in the opportunities of life. "And Jesus in the midst."

"Two thieves"—who, by evil doing had set, with their own wicked hands, the crown of infamy upon their own brows.

"And Jesus in the midst"—a spotless and innocent lamb between two snarling wolves.

"Two thieves"—the air hideous all around with invective, hearing the coarse mockeries, "cast the same in his teeth" (Matt. 27:44).

"And Jesus in the midst"—God's nightingale, with voice of love, between two puff adders with venom in their voices.

Amid the darkness, and louder than the crash of rocks loosened by earthquake, there were those concerning whom this was true:

> *"And they that passed by railed on him, wagging their heads, and saying, Ah, thou that destroyest the temple, and buildest it in three days, save thyself, and come down from the cross"*—MARK 15:29-30.

And of the chief priests it is written:

> *"Likewise also the chief priests mocking said among themselves with the scribes, He saved others; himself he can not save. Let Christ the King of Israel descend now from the cross, that we may see and believe"*
> —MARK 15:31-32.

"And Jesus in the midst"—holy recipient of their foul abuse.

"Two thieves"—any beautiful dreams they had ever had now moulded in the muck and mud and mess of their transgressions—standing on the border line of eternity, reviling him whom all the angels of God worship.

"And Jesus in the midst"—Rose of Sharon between two cactus plants.

"Two thieves"—all their years eaten by the locusts of evil, yawning pits of black despair before them.

"And Jesus in the midst"—a dove between two hissing serpents.

And one thief said:

> *"And one of the malefactors which were hanged railed on him, saying, If thou be Christ, save thyself and us"*
> —LUKE 23: 39.

Talmadge says of this:

"If thou be the Son of God." Was there any "if" about it? Tell me, thou star that in robe of light did run to point out his birthplace. Tell me, thou sea that didst put thy hand over thy lip when he bade thee be still. Tell me, thou sun in mid-heaven, who for him didst pull down over thy face thy veil of darkness. Tell me, ye lepers who were cleansed, ye dead who were raised, is he the Son of God? Aye! Aye! responds the universe. The flowers breathe it; the stars chime it; the redeemed celebrate it; the angels rise on their thrones to announce it. And yet on that miserable malefactor's "if" how many shall be wrecked for all eternity! That little "if" has enough venom in its sting to cause the death of a soul. No "if" about it. I know it. *Ecce Deus!* I feel it thoroughly—through every muscle of the body and through every faculty of my mind and through every energy of my soul. Living I will preach it; dying, I will pillow my head upon its consolations—Jesus, the God.

But, somehow, during these wild and wicked scenes, one thief had quickly and surely grown penitent. "As men who have been nearly drowned tell us that in one moment while they were under the water their whole life passed before them, so I suppose in one moment the dying malefactor thought over all his past life." He looked upon himself as a guilty wretch—as one who deserved to die. In that time of torment, he saw the sin and futility of blaspheming Christ who had done him no wrong. Yet the malefactor felt he could not die as he had lived—in sin and rebellion against God. The tortures of his guilty soul becoming more painful than the tortures of his boly, he saw his past as a scene of misdoing—saw himself as guilty of "the mightiest felony in the universe," for he had robbed God— had robbed God of his time and of his talent, robbed him of his service. And so—he spoke—answering the reviling and still impenitent comrade in crime:

> *"Dost not thou fear God, seeing thou art in the same condemnation? And we indeed justly; for we receive the due reward of our deeds: but this man hath done nothing amiss"*—LUKE 23:40-41.

And that dying, penitent thief, at the moment, saw Jesus as the friend of the outcast. He saw Jesus as the Lamb of God giving his life as a ransom for many! He saw Jesus as the One sent from God—to die. He saw Jesus as One who, in life, in death, proved that God's unfathomed love is greater than man's sin and folly—in life, in death,—proved that there is a wideness in God's mercy like the wideness of the sea. Yea, though the thief saw late, yet at last he saw.

This dying thief, looked upon by the crucifiers as merely dying vermin, looked upon as despicable dust which no man values, the ruined pivots and pulleys of his rending physical mechanism falling apart, maybe in his mind and heart a far-off vision of the Lake of Galilee and quiet hills and a home of peace whose threshold he shall cross no more, desires to fall asleep on some kind bosom. So, gazing upon the face of Christ, through the thickening gloom, he calls unto him somewhat as a wounded animal caught in the jaws of a steel trap wailingly appeals for help. He said:

> *"Lord, remember me when thou comest into thy kingdom"*—LUKE 23:42.

And, as he spoke, in praise, amid the mockings and
jeers of the mob, his was the one voice which attested
him Redeemer when all had forsaken him and fled. His
was the tortured voice which was the one note of sweetness in the wild, unmusical discord. His was the voice,
though the voice of a malefactor, for whose evil deeds
there is neither apology nor defense, which was the one
cry of faith in the hour of infinite denial and rejection.
So now we hear the impenitent thief railing—like a
hissing adder dying in the fire. And we hear the penitent
thief rebuking and praying.

One of the thieves dying in despair. The other coming out of his bondage, sorrow, and night into Christ's
freedom, gladness and light. One choosing the way that
leads to night and the dark dungeons of hell. The other
choosing the road that leads to light and the mansions
eternal in the heavens. One going to deeper depths of
ruin untold. The other coming out from the depths of
ruin untold into the peace of God's sheltering fold. What
a picture we have here of men today, some of whom
choose the way of destruction, some of whom choose the
way of eternal life. Some choose the deserts of a grow-
ing and eternal wasting—some the blossoming fields of
God's paradise. Some, living in the same place where
others are saved, choose the place where men and women
are "burning continually, yet unconsumed; forever wasting, yet enduring still; dying perpetually, yet never
dead." But some, like the thief who cried for mercy,
choose the place where death's shadows and sin's slime
and sorrow's sighs are never known. Some, like the railing thief, choose the rebuking thief, choose a throne
where with Christ they shall sit—and reign.

A thief—a penitent thief. Nothing behind him but the ashes of a wasted life; nothing before but the fires of an eternal hell! Nothing behind but the folly of a sinful life; nothing ahead but the horrors of a sinner's death. Nothing behind but blight; nothing ahead but night— the awful outer darkness! Nothing behind but error; nothing before but terror! Nothing behind but gloom; nothing ahead but doom! No angels of consolation will speak his name when he goes shuddering through the gates of death. Dark, very dark, it will be there. Dreadful, dreadfully dreadful, it will be there. Lonely, terribly lonely, it will be there. So—he puts all his tangled thoughts into one prayer—"Lord, remember me when thou comest into thy kingdom!" The cry it is of an utterly friendless man, a man to whom the loneliness of death is a most tremendous terror. Yet this thief, seeing him as Savior, cried out from the depths of a vast abyss: "Lord, remember me when thou comest into thy kingdom!"

But there is another there whose hidden glory bursts through the dark cloud that veiled it. Jesus—able, willing, mighty to save! Jesus—bearing our sins in his own body on the tree! Jesus! He refused the invitation of the mob to come down from the cross—to prove his divinity. And, out of the depths of an infinite love, which no waters can drown, no fires consume, no blizzards freeze, he reaches out to the rescue of the dying thief! Christ Jesus will enter the other world with this poor dying thief upon his bosom. Shall friend or angel of judgment claim this man's soul when it is Christ who justifies? Nay! Nay—never! For the thief saw him, hailed him as King—as Savior. Great faith that—blossoming like a lily in a desert! Wonderful faith

that—shining amid the world's unbelief like a sun at
midnight! Marvelous faith that—giving forth fragrance
like a full-blown rose in a garbage lot!

And so—there were three crosses and three who died
there that day on Calvary.

One died FOR sin. That one was Jesus.

One died IN sin. That one was the impenitent thief.

One died saved FROM sin. That one was the penitent
thief.

One died in LOVE. That one was Jesus.

One died in DESPAIR. That one was the impenitent
thief.

One died in FAITH. That one was the penitent thief.

One died a Benefactor. That one was Jesus.

One died a blasphemer. That one was the impenitent
thief.

One died a believer. That one was the penitent thief.

There were three trees planted in a row that day. And
all three bore fruit. One tree yielded poison—the tree
on which the impenitent malefactor died. One tree
yielded bitter aloes—aloes "bitter as coloquintida"—the
tree on which the penitent thief died, "his heart within
burnt like an aftertaste of sin to one whose memory
drinks and loathes the lee of shame and sorrow deeper
than the sea." One tree—the middle tree—bore the
beautiful apples of love. That was the tree on which
Jesus died. "Norway pine and tropical orange and
Lebanon cedar would not make so strange a grove as
this orchard of Calvary."

One tree yielded blossoms. That was the tree on which
the penitent thief gasped his last breath. One tree yielded
briars. That was the tree where the wretched criminal,
holding in his face the sorrow of that unblessed hour,

"turning around on his spikes to hiss at Jesus"—Jesus whose name sounds down the corridors of the centuries like the music of all choirs, visible and invisible, poured forth in one anthem. One tree yielded blood—blood "drawn from Immanuel's veins." And that, of course, was the tree on which Jesus died. One tree was the tree of rejection—the impenitent's tree. One tree was the tree of reception—the penitent's tree. One tree was the tree of redemption—the Savior's tree.

Let us close with some words of Talmadge in our ears and hearts: "I have shown you the right-hand cross and the left-hand cross. Now come to the middle cross. We have stood at the one, and found it yielded poison. We have stood at the other and found it yielded bitter aloes. Come now to the middle cross, and shake down apples of love. Uncover your head. You never saw so tender a scene as this. You may have seen father and mother die, or companion or child die, but never so affecting a scene as this. The railing thief looked from one way and saw only the right side of Christ's face. The penitent thief looked from the other way and saw the left side of Christ's face. But in the full blaze of Gospel light you see Christ's full face. It was a suffering face. Human hate had done its worst, and hell had hurled its sharpest javelin—and devils had vented their hottest rage, when, with every nerve in his body in torture and every fiber of his heart in excruciation, he died.

"To the middle cross look, that your souls may live. I showed you the right-hand cross in order that you might see what an awful thing it is to be unbelieving. I showed you the left-hand cross that you might see what it is to repent. Now I show you the middle cross that you may see what Christ has done to save your soul. Poets have sung its praise, sculptors have attempted to commemorate it in marble. Martyrs have clung to it in fire, and Christians, dying quietly in their beds, have leaned their heads against it. This hour may all our souls embrace it with an ecstasy of affection. Lay hold of that cross! Everything else will fail you. Without a strong grip on that you perish. Put your hand on that and you are safe, though the world swing from beneath your feet.

"Throw down at the foot of that middle cross sin, sorrow, life, death—everything. We are slaves; Christ gives deliverance to the captive. We are thirsty; Christ is the river of salvation to slake our thirst. We are hungry; Jesus says: 'I am the bread of life.' We are condemned to die; Christ says: 'Save that man from going down into the pit; I am the ransom.' We are tossed on the sea of trouble; Jesus comes over it, saying: 'It is I. Be not afraid.' We are in darkness; Jesus says: 'I am the Bright and Morning Star.' We are sick; Jesus is the 'Balm of Gilead.' We are dead; hear the shrouds rend and the grave hillocks heave as he cried: 'I am the resurrection and the life; he that believeth in me, though he were dead, yet shall he live.' We want justification; 'Being justified by faith we have peace with God through our Lord Jesus Christ.' We want to exercise faith; 'Believe in the Lord Jesus Christ, and thou shalt be saved.' I want to get from under condemnation; 'There is now therefore no condemnation to them who are in Christ Jesus.'"

"The dying thief rejoiced to see
That fountain in his day;
And there may I, though vile as he,
Wash all my sins away:
Wash all my sins away,
Wash all my sins away;
And there may I, though vile is he,
Wash all my sins away."

CHAPTER V

THE TWO HATREDS

"They hated me without cause"—JOHN 15:25.
"Thou hast loved righteousness, and hated iniquity"
—HEBREWS 1:9.

JESUS, God incarnate, God veiled in mortal flesh, spoke of how men hated him—and of how they could not hate him without hating God. Note these words:

> *"If the world hate you, ye know that it hated me before it hated you. If ye were of the world, the world would love his own: but because ye are not of the world, but I have chosen you out of the world, therefore the world hateth you. Remember the word that I said unto you, The servant is not greater than his lord. If they have persecuted me, they will also persecute you; if they have kept my saying, they will keep your's also. But all these things will they do unto you for my name's sake, because they know not him that sent me. If I had not come and spoken unto them, they had not had sin: but now they have no cloke for their sin. He that hateth me hateth my Father also"*—JOHN 15:18-23.

These words from the mighty and versatile pen of the great Koehne dropped into my mind one day—descriptive words which somehow cause me to think of the storms of hatred that raged around Jesus:

"From the window of my home I once saw the last act in the tragedy of a storm. Above the fields, the broken fence, the torn trees, the flooded streams, stretched the magnificent fury of the tempest. But, like the tragedy of Hamlet, when all grows serene and peaceful after the

hero dies, so the winds seemed to cling half fainting to
bush and flower until the last notes of the thunder song
were trumpeted back from the hills beyond the river far
away. The clouds folded and re-folded upon the western
sky, their angry lips fretted with lightnings which had
lost their beautiful wrath. Then, suddenly, unseen
fingers reached from the background, the storm cloud
was torn in the center, lifted, and a blazing arch appeared.
Then, from mysterious depths, the sun streamed forth.
In history, that storm cloud was Heathenism, that beautiful rich arch was Judaism, and the glory streaming
through to the present time, the Christian religion."

As we are told and as we believe, heathenism then was
humanity upon its face in despair—and Judaism was
humanity upon its knees praying and prophesying. Then,
in Christ, for the first time in human history, humanity
stood upon its feet. When Christ came the world's lips
were "feverish with delirium" and "religion was clasp-
ing hands with idolatry" and "the scepter was frozen
with the tyranny of impeached civilizations." Then came
Jesus—speaking as never man spoke, but the world had
ears dull of hearing. Our Saxon ancestors, their skins
grotesquely tattooed, drinking maddening wine from
human skulls, had no "gentle blood that did gentle man-
ners breed," but were as gentle as starving lions smelling
blood-soaked meat. Then came Jesus, God's Lamb, to
give his blood in vicarious atoning sacrifice. At the time
when Jesus came "out of the ivory palaces of heaven into
this world of woe," "the eagle of civilization, girded with
the night owl's drooping wing, was making a slow flight
through the darkness." And there was not a tongue on
the Tiber that was not fettered with tyranny. Then came
Jesus, strong Son of God, Sun of the soul, into the midst

of earth's night to give light. When came Jesus—speaking Koehnely now—the children of slaves were whelped in dungeons—and men were yoked with cattle, and women were the spoils of callous soldiers. Here and there, too, a throne's black shadow cursed the world while "a tiger's scowl upon a tyrant's face was all that was known of government." Then came Jesus—into the midst of earth's unrighteousness to bring righteousness. War, walking then, as always War travels, with bloody boots and grinningly tying crepe to multitudinous door knobs, was ready to roll sword-wheeled chariots into doomed cities. Then came Jesus into the midst of earth's strife to give peace—"breaking armies across his knees" and sinking navies by simply saying, "Put up thy sword." Kings and rulers, "throne bred monsters whose baby lips had nursed the tiger's milk of cruelty, whose coronets should have been a living serpent coiled around the brow, whose frightful ambitions were to exalt self," were in authority. Then came Jesus into the midst of earth's selfishness—earth's insanity of existence—making himself of no reputation, made in the likeness of men—teaching, by precept and by example, that they who would be greatest among men must be servant of all.

When Jesus "forsook the courts of everlasting day and chose with us a darksome house of clay," there were "funeral anthems wailing woefully in old Egypt," already on her way to become a shabby sexton of splendid tombs. And there was "a funeral wreath on the brow of Persia" while, on the whole earth, as Horace would express it, "wasting and a new troop of fevers had settled." Then came Jesus, into the midst of earth's death to give life, saying, with authority such as not one other had, "I am the resurrection and the life." And these words fell on a world the map of which was turned upside down. Athens, the brain of the world, was stupidly drunk with the wine of skepticism. The Gentile nations, loosing wild tongues and shaking clenched fists, confessed absolute ignorance of God. The Pharisees, making long prayers of pretense, represented legalism—the loveless letter of the law. The Sadducees, with their dogmatic negations, denied a divine hope to the travail of the ages, while many Jews had no dealings with the Samaritans save as they dealt with them as one who drives a dog from his steps. Then came Jesus, treating a leper with the kingly grace he did a Nicodemus, causing people to wonder at the gracious words which proceeded out of his mouth—reserving no great truth for some special occasion, telling a Samaritan harlot truths worthy the audience of a Plato. And, as saith the Scriptures, the common people heard him gladly. Thus Jesus, "who never wore a garland of chivalry," he who wandered homeless in a world where "the foxes had holes and the birds of the air had nests," re-established the home and family "upon foundations that wars and migrations and revolutions have never shaken." A Man of Sorrow, his tears, like seas, gather up the world's rivers of anguish. Yet he said, "My joy" and "My peace." Jesus, broad as the horizon, narrow as the multiplication table, when it comes to matters of right and righteousness, was as universal as the air and as sympathetic as the noonday. He was everything God loved—everything God approved. Everywhere and all the time his life was a life of incarnate holiness. He translated into his daily life every doctrine of his heavenly mind.

Yet —

JESUS WAS HATED!

"If the world hate you, ye know that it hated me before it hated you . . . . but now have they both seen and hated both me and my Father"—JOHN 15:18, 24.

The money changers, expert in illicit traffic and in oppression, despised the young Nazarene. The knotty lawyers, skillful in turning the law against the innocent, loved him as a wolf loves the man that entraps him. The scribes, buried in precedents and legalism, hated him. The infidel Sadducees, with their dogmatic negations, held him in contempt. The Greeks, with their wild mythologies, pitied him for his foolishness. The Orientals, with their mystic speculations, had no ears to hear his teaching. The Romans, with their gross materialism, considered what he said and did as the wild nightmare of a disordered brain. The priests, with their self-righteous creeds, abhorred him. The stately rabbis looking at him out of envious eyes, considered him the fly in their ointment. Kings of his day slighted him and the rich sometimes flouted him.

It was the hatred of wolves for the Lamb. It was the hatred of serpents for the dove. It was the hatred of soot for incarnate snow. It was the hatred of hypocrisy for genuineness. It was the hatred of falsehood for truth. It was the hatred of wickedness for holiness. It was the hatred of darkness for light. It was the hatred of dirt for chastity. It was the hatred of hell for heaven. It was the hatred of darkness for light. There was but one mind in many men and that was bent against Jesus.

"He is despised and rejected of men; a man of sorrows, and acquainted with grief: and we hid as it were our faces from him; he was despised, and we esteemed him not"—ISAIAH 53:3.

With this verse, Handel opens the second part of his great oratorio. It is said that at this point in its composition, Handel was found with his head upon the table weeping.

The birth of Jesus in Bethlehem was in poverty. Should poverty make them hate him? The poverty was like that of any other Jewish child. Should that make them hate him? He lived for thirty years in subjection to his mother and to Joseph. Should obedience to parents make them hate him? He was not stamped with the imprint of the schools. Should an educational matter cause them to hate him? He worked in Nazareth as a carpenter. Should one's honorable trade and environment cause hatred? He gathered his disciples, one here, another there, from the lowly order of society. Should one be hated because his followers are from obscure places? He paid tribute and custom—his taxes, if you please. Should one be hated for that? He showed respect to every constituted authority. Should one be hated for the fruit of good citizenship? He said nothing about the rights of the people or the claims of the Jewish race —believing that "no man has a right to all his rights." But is holy silence a just cause for hatred?

Although temptations never loosened a fibre of his being, hatred prodded him. Though in love he made persuasive appeal by a dedicated and outpoured life, there were hate mongers who had but one mind in them, and that was bent against Jesus. Though he went about doing good, they hated him. "For which of my works do ye stone me?"

"Then the Jews took up stones again to stone him. Jesus answered them, Many good works have I shewed you from my Father; for which of those works do ye stone

me? The Jews answered him saying, For a good work we stone thee not; but for blasphemy; and because that thou, being a man, makest thyself God. Jesus answered them Is it not written in your law, I said, Ye are gods? If he called them gods, unto whom the word of God came, and the scripture can not be broken; say ye of him, whom the Father hath sanctified, and sent into the world, Thou blasphemest; because I said, I am the Son of God? If I do not the works of my Father, believe me not. But if I do, though ye believe not me, believe the works: that ye may know, and believe, that the Father is in me, and I in him. Therefore they sought to take him: but he escaped out of their hands"
—JOHN 10:31-39.

Though many never constructed a torture rack for him, they had torture-rack attitudes in their hearts. Though many never tried to burn him at the stake, there were hellish fires of hatred in their hearts. Though many never tried to put him in prison, they had prison-bar hatred in their hearts. Though many never rose up to do him violence, they had insurrections in their hearts against him. In the hearts of men there were revolts of hatred against Jesus, revulsions of hatred. Truly, the heart of man was a council chamber of devils, the egg out of which was hatched the plots of hatred and the maliciousness of murder. Some who hated each other, rotten and vile and abominably low, became friends in mutual hatred of Jesus. Remember what is said of Pilate and King Herod:

"And the same day Pilate and Herod were made friends together: for before they were at enmity between themselves"—LUKE 23:12.

"The kings of the earth stood up, and the rulers were gathered together against the Lord, and against his

Christ. For of a truth against thy holy child Jesus, whom thou hast anointed, both Herod and Pontius Pilate, with the Gentiles, and the people of Israel, were gathered together"—ACTS 4:26-27.

The hissing mob said: "We have no king but Caesar!" In substance they said: A king? Then a crown he must have. So they crowned him with a crown of thorns.

A king? Then the insignia of his high office he needs. So, with the merciless scourge, they seamed his quivering flesh until it started up in red scars.

A king? Then we must give testimony of our allegiance. So they spat in his face.

A king? Then we must raise and reach our hands to him. So they beat him with their fists, slapped him with hard palms, pulled out his beard.

A king? Then regal robes he must wear. So they, with studied indignity, put on him a purple robe.

A king? Then a scepter he ought to have. So they, in vulgar jest, put a reed in his hand.

A king? Then a proclamation must be made. So they bowed the knee in jest and scoffingly said, "Hail, King of the Jews!"

A king? Then he ought to have a coronation psalm. So they, with rabble-frenzy, cried out, "Crucify him!"

A king? Then a right royal procession he must have. So they led him, as a lamb to the slaughter, to Golgotha.

A king? Then he ought to have a throne. So they lifted him upon a wooden cross, himself nailed thereon.

A king? Then he ought to have a chalice. So they gave him a sponge filled with vinegar and gall. He bowed to every oppression. He submitted meekly to every indignity. Though he is Alpha and Omega and all lovely names, though his is the sweetest name ever on mortal tongue—they called him glutton, winebibber, liar, buffoon, deceiver, bastard, blasphemer, devil.

He died in great agony—the object of priestly hatred. They wagged their heads and mocked him on the cross in hatred. "Spleen to mankind their envious hearts possessed." And "much they hated others, but most they hated the best." Against Jesus rose "the unleavened hatred of their hearts"—planting hatred of long duration in the hearts of others. The depth of their hatred is set forth in Isaiah 49:7:

> *"Thus saith the Lord, the Redeemer of Israel, and his Holy One, to him whom man despiseth, to him whom the nation abhorreth, to a servant of rulers, Kings shall see and arise, princes also shall worship, because of the Lord that is faithful, and the Holy One of Israel, and he shall choose thee."*

An Israel's blind hatred of the Messiah did not stop short at his person, or his virgin mother, but extended to his words and works. His works were (and still are among many Jews) ascribed to witchcraft and Beelzebub. This hatred is incomprehensible. The mystery of it is set forth in the words of our Lord: "They hated me without cause." Though he offered every blessing to men, they multiplied their insults against him, the only Savior, the only life. They preferred their sins with all their consequences, to their God.

And are any who listen now numbered among those who hated him? Is not a rejection by neglect or by indifference or by disobedience or by doubt just as much a rejection as the rejection of hate? In every land billions of tons of armaments piled high. In every land multiplying shells and guns. In every land stores of poison gas and bombs. In many lands skies darkened by death-dealing planes. In some lands children taught from their cradles to bluster and hate, to strut in military parade; when they could scarcely walk, to nurse a rifle as though it were a cherished toy.

Everywhere the blind surges of mankind. Everywhere the restless plunges into momentary pleasure. Everywhere the fevered strivings for material gain. And over all, amid the sound of jazz and clinking coin, we see the omnipresent ghastly dread, the approaching specter of self-created doom. Thus we take our stand with those who hated him while we sing "My Jesus, I love Thee." "This lovely, fruitful earth, overflowing with plenty, riven from end to end by hate, oppression and brutal cruelty, which, if unchecked, must surely crumble civilization to dust. And less than twenty-five years ago nine million men yielded up their lives to save humanity!"

And across our minds is endless talk by voices of incompetence, endless explanations advanced by human ingenuity. The talk of economic stress, of boom and slump, depression and recession, unemployment and unrest—the rise and fall of nations, the need for colonies, the survival of the fittest—fatuous and futile jabberings, which only people dumb as a doll on a ventriloquist's knee could believe.

But there is only one basic explanation—only one reason. Men have forgotten God. Millions now living are blind and deaf—dead indeed—to the knowledge of their Creator. For countless human souls the Name above every name is nothing but myth. For others an inherited tradition to which lip service must be paid. For others a convenient oath. For others bland hypocrisy. False gods as evil as the golden calf now stand upon the altars of many professing Christians.

Are those who hated him in the long ago, the only sailors on this ship of rejection? Are those who spat upon him any more guilty than those who are ashamed of him in this delirious world? These words are not so much instruction as they are a warning lest we voyage on the sea of rejection with those who by hatred rejected him long ago.

But within that last week the public ministry of our Lord Jesus was unimpeachable evidence of —

GOD'S HATRED OF SIN.

"God is love." But God is also a God of hate.

> *"Thou lovest righteousness, and hatest wickedness"*
> —PSALMS 45:7.

'Tis true that "the greatest hate springs from the greatest love." God could not love sinners so deeply did he not hate sin so greatly. I think just here of two lines —

> *"Dante, who loved well because he hated,*
> *Hated wickedness that hinders loving."*

Many are the words and events of the Bible that teach God's hatred of sin and all unrighteousness. But the cross alone—the bloody center of all events of that week —shows how much and how eternally God hates sin. Sin, life's most dreadful and inexorable curse. Sin, so like a river, beginning in a quiet spring, ending in a tumultous sea. Sin—the desert breath that drinks up every dew. Sin—the death head set amidst life's feast. Sin—the power that reversed man's nature, destroyed the harmony of his powers, threw him, woefully deranged, miserable, ungoverned, erratic, lost, into interminable leagues of night. Sin—the evil that subverted the con-

stitutional order of his nature, dismantled him of his
nobility, brought him in unconditional surrender to
diabolical power, caused him treacherously to give up the
keys of the soul's citadel placed in his keeping.

We can not drown the stench of sin's carrion under
flood-tides of philosophical perfume. Sin, a fatal mis-
chief of the heart, a seed big with future pain and grief,
the quintessence of all horrors, the causative element of
all world suffering, is no whirlwind creating a slight dis-
turbance, but a hot sirocco blasting all gardens. No light
discord— a thunderbolt that shatters the organ into
splinters, leaving it without shape or tone. No pen knife
—a guillotine. No slight jerk of the hiccoughs—the
agonies of sciatica. No lame Mephibosheth—a diabolical
Jezebel. No crude catapult—a bursting bomb. No quiet
pool—a maelstrom. No cool rill—a perpetual lava rush
scorching its way through green fields.

When we look at sin with regard to God we say that
sin must be "the greatest evil which is most opposite to
the greatest good." Sin, the nightmare of the human race,
is ignorance, folly, madness, blindness, deafness, sick-
ness, poison, slavery, plague, death, hell. As it is said
of Nabal, "as the name is, so is the man"—the same may
be observed of sin. For "as the name is, so is the thing."
For what term is there, expressible of reproach or misery
—what image is there that can produce aversion or fear,
that is not employed by the Scriptures to represent sin?
Sin is not libelled by any image or term, no matter how
hideous and horrible, used to describe it. Sin substan-
tially contains all evils—and is the cause of all. Sin is
the fountain head which has embittered all our streams
—and the seed which has so thickly sown the world with
wretchedness. Therefore, it is never libelled by any of

its dreadful representations. Because of sin, man, at his birth, enters a labyrinth of thorns and briars and can not move without "piercing himself through with many sorrows."

Behold Adam and Eve expelled from Paradise! Behold the deluge of Noah's day—sweeping away the world of the ungodly! Behold Sodom and Gomorrah—"set forth as an example suffering the vengeance of eternal fire"! Consider the plagues of Egypt. Consider the destruction of the former inhabitants of Canaan! Consider the dispersion and misery of the Jews—"the chosen people of God." In all these instances and in many more, the evil of sin is brought down to a level with our senses.

Moreover, it is sin that has reduced the material creation to vanity, and doomed it to a general conflagration. As, under the law, the house of the leper was to be pulled down, so it is with regard to this world. The day of God cometh wherein "the heavens shall pass away with a great noise, and the elements shall melt with fervent heat, the earth also and all the works that are therein, shall be burned up." And what place is that where "the smoke of their torment ascendeth up forever and ever"? In answering that question, forget not that sin built hell, that sin produced "the worm that never dies," that sin kindled "the fire that shall never be quenched."

But we must not forget that sin is enmity against God, against his attributes, against his government. God never yet revealed a design which sin hath not withstood. God has never given a command which sin has not trampled under foot. Sin deposes God from his sovereignty. Sin abuses God's goodness. Sin abhors God's holiness. Sin villifies God's wisdom. Sin insults and denies God's omniscience, his justice, his power. Sin makes a universal abuse. It would pull God from his throne. Sin abuses God's authority—authority interposed in his law. Sin abuses God's justice—as if God would not punish. Sin abuses God's power—as if God would wink at man's wickedness. Sin abuses God's law —as if God's law were not right and reasonable. Sin is an abuse of God's wisdom—as if God did not see and observe. Sin is an abuse of God's long-suffering patience and forbearance—as if God's Spirit would always strive with men. Sin is an abuse of God's threatening—as if God's threatenings were not to be feared. Sin is an abuse of God's promises—as if they were not to be regarded. Sin is an abuse of God's holiness—a direct contrariety to his nature and will. Sin is an abuse of Christ—an abuse of his nature and person and offices—his death, his blood, his righteousness—a refusing and a rejecting of him and his great salvation. It is such a universal abuse of God, Father, Son, and Holy Ghost, that no wonder they that see sin with the Psalmist, cry out with him— saying:

> *"Against thee, thee only, have I sinned, and done this*
> *evil in thy sight: that thou mighest be justified when*
> *thou speakest, and be clear when thou judgest"*
> —Psalms 51:4.

When sin thus abuses God in heaven, no wonder that it abuses men on earth. Your sin—man, woman—is an abuse of your rational soul, which is capable of glorious enjoyment in heaven, but by sin that soul grovels on earth among dust, wallows in a filthy kennel. Sin is an abuse of the body which should be the temple of the Holy Ghost, but by sin that body becomes the temple of the devil, whose second choice is a hog. Sin is an abuse and destruction of time, that precious time that should be used in preparing for eternity. It is an abuse of health and strength—and you employ them against God.

Sin is an abuse of riches—of wealth and worldly prosperity.

> *"But Jeshurun waxed fat, and kicked: thou art waxen fat, thou art grown thick, thou art covered with fatness; then he forsook God which made him, and lightly esteemed the Rock of his salvation"*—DEUT. 32:15.

> *"How shall I pardon thee for this? thy children have forsaken me, and sworn by them that are no gods: when I fed them to the full, they then committed adultery, and assembled themselves by troops in the harlots' houses. They were as fed horses in the morning: every one neighed after his neighbor's wife. Shall I not visit for these things? saith the Lord: and shall not my soul be avenged on such a nation as this?"*
> —JER. 5:7-9.

> *"For she did not know that I gave her corn and wine, and oil, and multiplied her silver and gold, which they prepared for Baal'*—HOSEA 2:8.

Thus we see how sin abuses God in men's use of material blessings. Some give most of the silver and gold that cometh to them, by the blessing of God upon them, to profane diversions, idle, vain, and wanton amusements —lewd and wicked practices.

Sin is an abuse of the preached word, the written word. It makes men wrest the Scriptures to their destruction, to impugn the necessity of divine revelation and turn deists, atheists, and incarnate devils. It is an abuse and destruction of wit, reason, talents, sermons, sabbaths, and everything.

Satan acts like a creeping dragon and then like a flying serpent. His first request seems mannerly and modest, as Semiramis desired of Ninus to reign but one day, and that day to do what she pleased—and that day she cut off his head. That's sin! Sin deceives man till man is hardened through its deceitfulness. It appears at first but little in the fountain, in the heart and thought; then it bubbles into a stream of evil words; then it increases into a revel of evil actions. Next it swells into a torrent and overflows till it drowns men in perdition.

Giving thought to the things we have just said, we can now say that we know assuredly that God hates sin. By every thorn that punctured Christ's brow; by every scar left by the merciless scourge; by every drop of blood "drawn from Emmanuel's veins"; by every breath he drew, which was a pang of pain; by every beat of his heart, which was a throb of agony; by every minute of that supernatural darkness which shrouded the world; by the offering of his sinless soul for sinful men, you know, I know, we all know, that God hates sin. And, oh, that we, seeing sin through the crimson lenses of Calvary's Cross, would hate sin, too!

"Greater love hath no man than this that a man lay down his life for his friend." But you were not his friends. "The mind of the flesh is enmity against God." No sacrifice can match Christ's, for he died for his enemies, for the weak, for the ungodly—for those who hated him. The sinless Son of God took the place of sinners, who hated him, and suffered their merited stroke that the penalty of sin might not be theirs. Have you contemplated the Cross? You will never find its match in the history of the universe of God. Do you appreciate the Cross? It stands peerless and alone. That is the place where Christ endured the separation from God which we deserved, that we might enjoy the nearness to God which he deserved.

Have you studied the cross? Study it! Then your soul will be overwhelmed with the mystery, the majesty, the marvel, the measure, the might of it. There is not in heaven or earth such an amazing wonder as this. Have you looked earnestly at the cross? All the promises of God are centered in that cross. All the happiness and good of man are centered in that cross.

Here the vilest sinner, the moment he receives Christ by faith, is accepted of God. Come to the cross with your poverty—and be enriched. If he is your physician —you shall have health. If he is your bread—you shall never hunger. If he is your fountain of life—you shall never thirst. If he is your light—you shall never abide in darkness. If he is your joy—you shall never remain in sorrow. If he is your truth—you shall never be led astray. If he is your righteousness—who shall condemn you? If he is your sanctification—who shall reject you? If he is your acquittal—who shall sentence you?

Come to the cross with your death—and get his life. Come to the cross with your ruin—and get his perfection. Come to the cross with your sin—and get his righteousness. Come to the cross with your bitterness—and get his sweetness. Come to the cross with your despair— and get his assurance. Come to the cross with your darkness—and get his light. Come to the cross with your sorrow—and get his joy. And then say:

> *"When I survey the wondrous Cross,*
> *On which the Prince of Glory died,*
> *My richest gain I count but loss,*
> *And pour contempt on all my pride."*

Chapter VI

THE TWO NIGHTS

*"And it shall come to pass in that day, saith the Lord
God, that I will cause the sun to go down at noon, and
I will darken the earth in the clear day"*—Amos 8:9

*"And it was about the sixth hour, and there was a dark-
ness over all the earth until the ninth hour. And the
sun was darkened"*—Luke 23:44-45.

A DAY has but one morning—whether it be morning
"in russet mantle clad, walking o'er the dew of eastern
hills," whether it be "morning fair with pilgrim steps in
amice grey," whether it be morning which "like a lobster
boiled, from black to red begins to turn," whether it be
morning which is "the babbling eastern scout, the nice
morn on the Indian steep from her cabin loop-hole peep-
ing." A day has but one morning—not two—whether it
come quietly like the flow of an unruffled stream or
thunderously in clouds that make the sun's chariot seem
to run slowly. Whether the morning hour has gold in
its mouth or rain in its mouth, still the day hath but one
morn.

And every day has but one night—whether that night
be "a fearful night with danger on the deep," whether
"'tis a naughty night to swim in" or a night "almost at
odds with morning," whether it be

> *"A comfort-killing night, image of hell,*
> *Dim registry and notary of chance,*
> *Black stage for tragedies and murders fell—*
> *Vast sin-concealing chaos, nurse or blame!"*

The day has but one night whether it come "gray-hooded, like a sad votarist in palmer's weed" or as "a sable goddess from her ebon throne, in rayless majesty, stretching forth her leaden sceptre o'er a slumbering world." The day has but one night even if we can speak of it and say:

> "Beautiful night!
> A dewy freshness fills the silent air;
> No mist obscures, nor cloud, nor speck, nor stain,
> Breaks the serene of heaven."

Every day has but one night even if we can describe it thus:

> "O stormy night!
> I see a brimstone sea of boiling fire,
> And fiends, with knotted whips of flaming wire,
> Torturing poor souls, that gnash their teeth in vain,
> And gnaw their flame-tormented tongues for pain."

Though all centuries rise up and say they never had a day that had two nights, yet must the centuries make one exception. For once, in the long ago "a dull rumble of thunder rolled out of the desert of Tekoa—out of the desert, in the voice of a man—a man bearded, browned, afire." And that man's name was Amos—"God's thunder over Israel, the thunder prelude to the gathering storm, the first fighting picket of a new battalia of prophets." With eyes and lips that threw flame, he, at a time when the soul of religion was divorced from morality, at a time when "the outside of the cup was polished gold and the inside tarnished and foul," excoriated the rich for "selling the righteous for silver" and the poor for a pair of shoes."

And, burningly vivid, like a flash of zig-zag lightning that rips open the vestments of a storm cloud, is one sentence that shows the one exception of the centuries—the one day with two nights:

> *"And it shall come to pass in that day, saith the Lord God, that I will cause the sun to go down at noon, and I will darken the earth in the clear day"*—Amos 8:9

That is what Amos said that God said. And here is how God—after eight hundred years—verified that prophecy as true:

> *"Now from the sixth hour there was darkness over all the land unto the ninth hour"*—Matt. 27:45.

According to Jewish reckoning the sixth hour was noon. And the ninth hour was three in the afternoon. "The third hour"—nine o'clock in the morning—they crucified him. "The sixth hour"—twelve o'clock—noon time—there was darkness—darkness,

> *"Dark as was chaos, ere the infant Sun*
> *Was rolled together, or had tried his beams*
> *Athwart the profound gloom."*

"There was darkness"! Darkness—"dark as misery's woeful night," "dark as a murderer's mask of crepe," and "cold like a benighted hemisphere." "There was darkness over all the land"—darkness, "dark as the parentage of chaos," "dark as the caves wherein earth's thunders groan," "dark as the helmsman's bark of old that ferried to hell the dead," "dark as the shroudings of a bier, as if the blessed atmosphere was dim." "All around was darkness like a wall."

Out yonder that strange day somewhere, a plowman—and darkness settles down on his furrows. Out yonder on the lake somewhere, a fisherman—and night comes down at noon. He who was and is THE LIGHT OF THE WORLD, hanging in darkness. He who said "I am the Light of the world; he that followeth me shall not walk in darkness, but shall have the light of life"—hanging there with none to follow—on his death-bed of four spikes, two for the hands and two for the feet.

Jesus, the Bright and Morning Star, hanging in darkness.

Jesus, the Sun of Righteousness, hanging in darkness.

Jesus, Light of light, crying from out the darkness, "My God, my God, why hast thou forsaken me?"

Jesus, who, in creation wisdom and power, sent the first ray of light speeding like some archangel with garments of fire across the uncharted dark of chaos, dying in darkness.

He that sent forth Acturus and opened the golden gates of the first morning—now bleeding in darkness—with midnight coming down at noonday.

Jesus, who set the sun in a tabernacle, in the high heavens, now the bleeding One on a skull-shaped hill. O, what a day was that!

> *"Well might the sun in darkness hide*
> *And shut his glories in,*
> *When Christ, the mighty Maker, died,*
> *For man, the creature's sin."*

Midnight came at noonday—midnight when the stars, those pitiless, passionless eyes that burn man's nothingness into man, kept sentinel duty in those battle-fields where once the stars in their course fought against

Sisera. At noonday, midnight came—midnight, the outlaw's day; midnight, when even an atheist half believes in God, when the veil between the frail present and the eternal future grows thin, when the moon glows like a huge yellow cameo on the breast of the sky. And out yonder, as midnight came at noontime, some night bird with weird and discordant cry, as though it spoke of the wild and awful scenes enacted, uttered its wail. And in the valley of Jehoshaphat some skulking beast, as though it knew of the crimson terrors on the skull-shaped hill, snarled with tones akin to those of the men who hooted and howled around the cross.

But this was no eclipse. For the Passover comes near full moon—a time when a solar eclipse is impossible. It was no eclipse—because no total solar eclipse lasts three hours. It was no eclipse—because no eclipse ever covers a whole land. God had said:

> *"And it shall come to pass in that day . . . that I will cause the sun to go down at noon, and I will darken the earth in the clear day"*—AMOS 8:9.

Thus God's word authenticates itself. Thus the prophecy of Amos—so literally fulfilled in one person—appeals to every honest person as one of the undeniable proofs that the Scripture can be none other than the inspired word of God.

As this supernatural darkness must have been dreadful, so is the spiritual, eternal "outer darkness" at the end of a Christless life. This darkness was typical of the powers of darkness seeming to prevail—of the sufferings of Jesus, the despair of the disciples.

But today he whose life-light seemed to come down to the feeble flickerings of a candle on that dark day, now blazes like the sun in mid-heavens tabernacled. Therefore, come to that Light!

> "*The whole world was lost in the darkness of sin,*
> *The Light of the world is Jesus;*
> *Like sunshine at noonday His glory shone in,*
> *The Light of the world is Jesus.*
>
> "*No darkness have we who in Jesus abide,*
> *The Light of the world is Jesus;*
> *We walk in the Light when we follow our Guide,*
> *The Light of the world is Jesus.*
>
> "*Ye dwellers in darkness with sinblinded eyes,*
> *The Light of the world is Jesus;*
> *Go, wash, at His bidding, and light will arise,*
> *The Light of the world is Jesus.*
>
> "*No need of the sunlight in heaven we're told,*
> *The Light of the world is Jesus;*
> *The Lamb is the Light of the City of God,*
> *The Light of that world is Jesus.*
>
> "*Come to the Light, 'tis shining for thee;*
> *Sweetly the Light has dawned upon me;*
> *Once I was blind, but now I can see;*
> *The Light of the world is Jesus.*"

Jesus said:

> "*I am the light of the world: he that followeth me shall not walk in darkness, but shall have the light of life*"
> —JOHN 8:12.

Jesus also said:

> "*Ye are the light of the world*"—MATT. 5:14.

Showing what? Teaching us what? Just what Jesus said:

> *"Peace be unto you: as my Father hath sent me, even so send I you."*—JOHN 20:21.

He has sent us to be light—to others.

Even when we consider the wonders of light we get only a faint conception of what Jesus, the Light of the world, is! Light travels at the rate of one hundred and eighty-six thousand miles per second—and yet it is not a substance. It moves at that speed seven times around the world in the tick of a clock, and yet it is not a substance. It is a process and carried on by some media of which we know but little. Light is a vibration, yet, though passing through the vibrations of the air, it is not carried by the vibrations of the air, for the vibrations of the air are *one million* times slower than the vibrations of light. Moreover light comes by vertical vibrations while air has only horizontal vibrations. The media upon which light vibrations travel is capable of penetrating crystals and probably opague substances, yet not a substance. Again, in its movements through these solids it is not carried by the vibrations of the solids, but by something whose vibrations are many times more rapid than the vibrations of the substance through which it passes.

Go where you will and the fertilizing wonder of light confronts you. In the sky above, in the earth beneath, in the deeps under the earth, you are ever in the presence of the begetting power of light. "Every lump of coal is a clot of the sun's blood turned black. Every little brown seed that has wakened to life in the long, long history of the past, every spring of grass that has climbed out of its tiny grave and has become an emerald string upon which the south wind plays a resurrection melody, every tree that has thrown out its branches as so many begging hands to be filled with treasure from the atmosphere, all the animal life that has come and gone— all represent the bloody sweat and aching agony of the sun."

Now light is the secret of all that is fair and beautiful in earth, in sea, in sky. The thousand-featured creation says: "I am what I am because light is what it is." Imagine this earth without the sun. "The fields would droop; houses would be as sepulchers; business would be hushed in the street! The banker would forget his bank; the mechanic his tools, the merchant his goods, the farmer his plow, the seekers of pleasure their places of resort! The sail would hang at rest in the harbor! There would be no light; nothing could grow; nothing could blossom; there would be no color in the flowers, none in the sky, none in pictures, none in the living human face; life itself would be dead; and the world would be buried. If the sun were lost to us, then the moon and the stars, also, would cease to appear; for they shine only as the sun shines upon them. No sun! No moon! No stars! Then there could be no succession of day and night— night and day! All must be an unbroken, awful darkness! Life-destroying damps! Death-dealing miasmas! No light to penetrate and purify! The mind may attempt to fill up the picture of the earth's condition, if the sun, the king of day, should disappear from our horizon."

But how terribly tragic—how infinitely worse would be the condition of the human world without Christ, the King of glory, the Sun of Righteousness. How glorious the assurance that those who follow him "shall not walk in darkness, but shall have the light of life." More than the sun is to the physical world is Christ to the spiritual world. As there can be no physical life unless the sun gives its light, so there can be no spiritual life, unless it be produced by the light of Christ. He is the source of all true religious *light*—and so of all true religious *life*. The light that falls from Christ upon the man who follows him will give life that shall know no end. He will have a light that grows brighter and brighter, till it blazes into perfect day. Once I heard a good man say something like this:

"There are different temperaments in the world. But through Jesus and his transforming and redeeming and justifying grace each and all who give him a chance at their hearts and lives produce the beautiful and wonderful! The sun falls upon the prairies of Minnesota—and the soil answers with wheat. The sun falls on the soil of the South—and the South answers with cotton. The sun falls on the fields of Cuba—and Cuba answers with sugar. The sun falls on the soil of California and California answers with fruit. The sun says to the violet, 'Here is abundance; take what you will.' And the violet takes a little light and returns perfume. Just as the oak takes much light and returns ship timber." So Christ, the Light of the world, came giving life as the summer-making sun!

And now—in conclusion—let me say that he who follows Jesus Christ, the Light of the world, will be guided into that haven of eternal rest and joy. I speak, as you quickly see, of heaven. The hope of heaven is bound up with the dearest and tenderest and most sacred things of my life. It is a part of myself. If I miss heaven— think how much I shall miss! If I miss heaven—how utterly worthless will be everything else that I have called

my own. My mother who stood to me as my best inter-
pretation of God since my baby days and sent me her
blessing from her death-bed, beside the sunset sea, is in
heaven. My father who stands before me today as old
Samuel of Gilgal, who would suffer his right arm cut
off before he would cheat a single man or refuse to pay
a debt he owed, and whose dying breath, like the last
whisper of a storm that spent itself, is in heaven. Many
of the dearest friends I have, men and women for whom
I would have died and who would have as willingly died
for me, are in heaven. I can never see them again outside of heaven! If I miss heaven, I miss them all. God
help me, I must be there!

What will making a fortune amount to—if I miss
heaven? What will gaining fame amount to—if I miss
heaven? What will gaining a bit more temporary applause
be worth—if I miss heaven? How can the gain of the
world repay me for the loss of heaven? If you were to
give me all the millions of the Rockefellers and the Fords
and give me all the honor of all the kings and the states-
men poured into one goblet of fame—what would it be
worth if I miss heaven? If you were to give me all the
luxury and all the ease of all the palaces of earth con-
densed for one human body to rest upon and revel in,
for the few short years it is possible for me to live on
this earth, what beggar's rags, what ashes, what trash,
what tawdry pearls of paste, they would be compared to
the hope of heaven and the meeting there in eternal re-
union and fellowship with those, redeemed by his blood,
who have gone on before. God help us—we must not
miss heaven!

We can miss money—if we must. We can miss
worldly success—if we must. We can miss honor and

praise—if we must. We can endure hardships—if necessary. We can bear burdens—if necessary. But we must not miss heaven!

Led by Christ who is the Light of the world, walking in the light as he is in the light, letting our light so shine before men that they may see our good works and glorify our father who is in heaven, we shall come, one of God's days, to the city of light—a city whose light Jesus *is*.

"And the city had no need of the sun, neither of the moon, to shine in it: for the glory of God did lighten it, and the Lamb is the light thereof. And the nations of them which are saved shall walk in the light of it"
—REV. 21:23-24.

CHAPTER VII

THE TWO RENDINGS

"And the rocks rent" —MATT. 27:51.

"And, behold, the veil of the temple was rent in twain from the top to the bottom" —MATT. 27:51.

WHEN people have spoken of rocks and mountains, they have spoken words like these: "What is more hard than *rock?* What is softer than the wave? Yet hard rocks are hollowed by the soft water" — as Virgil — "they attack this one man with their hate and their shower of weapons. But he is like *some rock* that stretches into the vast sea, and which, exposed to the fury of the winds and beaten against by the waves, endures all the violence and threats of heaven and sea, himself standing unmoved."

And this — by Milton:

> *"Rifted rocks whose entrance leads to hell,*
> *For such there be, but unbelief is blind."*

And this — from an old song:

> *"Under floods that are deepest,*
> *Which Neptune obey,*
> *Over rocks that are steepest,*
> *Love will find out the way,*
> *Love will find out the way."*

And this — from Sir Walter Scott:

> *"The rock summits, split and rent,*
> *Formed turret, dome, or battlement,*
> *Or seemed fantastically set*
> *With cupule or minaret."*

And this — by Masefield:

> *"And all night long the stone*
> *Felt how the wind was blown;*
> *And all night long the rock*
> *Stood the sea's shock;*
> *While, from the window, I*
> *Looked out and wondered why,*
> *Why at such length*
> *Such force should fight and strength."*

But the rocks do not sin. But one day, the rocks, less hard than were the hearts of wicked men, were rent asunder at the death of. Jesus. And an earthquake, as unforeseen to science as an eclipse is calculable by science, rolled forth his dirge. "And the rocks rent." It was the rocks saluting the Rock of Ages. It was the dust worshipping him who would never be dust. The hard rocks—less hard, less callous, less icy, less insensitive than were the hearts of some who had part in doing him to death—rent, split open. But it is of the rent veil we would have you think now—prayerfully, worshipfully, gratefully.

Now there were miracles which attended or preceded the death and burial of Jesus. We are told that "the earth did quake, and the rocks rent, and the graves were opened, and many bodies of the saints which slept arose." Though men could bestow little honor upon his funeral, the heavens bestowed marks of honor—adorned it with divers miracles, which "lessened the reproach of his death." We have already mentioned the extraordinary and supernatural darkness—when "the sun fainted at the sight of such a rueful spectacle and clothed the whole heaven in black." Flavel says that the sight of this caused a great philosopher, who was then far from the place where this unparalleled tragedy was acting, to cry out, *Aut Deus natura patitur, aut mundi machina dissolvitur* —"either the God of Nature now suffers, or the frame of the world is dissolved." We think, too, of the earth-quake and of the graves that opened and of the dead bodies of many saints who arose and went into the holy city, and were seen of many. The rending of the rocks was a sign of God's fierce indignation (Naham 1:6) and manifested the greatness of his power—showing what men deserved and what God could do to them who had committed this horrid deed. Though God rather chose at this time to show the deed upon inanimate rocks than upon rock-hearted sinners, especially the deed served to convince the world that it was none other than the Son of God who died. But that which is put in the first rank of these miracles is that "the veil of the temple was rent in twain." This event, a great event among miraculous events, stands above other events as a high mountain above high mountains. We find the evangelist Mark mentions this in particular—and none of the other of these miracles does he mention—as if this rending of the veil were the miracle most to be noticed, as containing somewhat mysterious and significant therein.

> *"And Jesus cried with a loud voice, and gave up the ghost. And the veil of the temple was rent in twain from the top to the bottom"*—MARK 15:37-38.

A full and entire rent of the veil it was. Luke says it "was rent in the midst." Matthew and Mark say it "was rent in twain"—rent from the top to the bottom—an entire rent. It was a notable miracle, for at that very instant when the veil was rent, the high priest was officiat-ing in the most holy place. Then the veil which hid him from the rest of the people was rent from top to bottom —like Christ's flesh, and torn aside. And what was the veil? That was the great veil which stretched across the temple between the holy place where the priests ministered in their *daily* service and the Holy of Holies into which only the high priest entered *once a year* with the *blood* offering for the sins of the people. We are told that this holy of holies was a perfect cube of fifteen feet into which no ray of outside light ever entered—wherein rested the Ark of the Covenant with the mercy seat and all that was inside the Ark of the Covenant. The mercy-seat of that Ark signified Christ, the great propitiation. The pot of manna inside that Ark signified Christ, the Bread of life.

Edersheim tells us that the veil which hid the Holy Place (where the priests ministered DAILY from the Holy of Holies, where the high priest went only once a YEAR) was fifty feet long by thirty feet wide by four inches thick— made of seventy-two squares of richest embroidery in which there was not one black thread and so heavy that it required three hundred priests to manipulate it. Behind this veil, as we have it presented to us in Leviticus 16, the high priest, having caught in a basin the blood from the riven heart of the sacrificial lamb (or goat), hastened with the blood, without delay, behind the veil into the Holy of Holies and sprinkled that blood upon the mercy seat to make atonement. This was the veil that was rent asunder from top to bottom.

It was, as those wiser than we have said, in conformity to the temple of Christ's body which was now dissolved. Christ was the true temple, in whom dwells all the fulness of the Godhead bodily. When in agony and yet in triumph he cried and gave up the ghost, and so dissolved and rent the veil of his flesh, the literal temple did, as it were, echo the cry, and answer the strokes by rending its veil.

Showing what? Showing that all ceremonies were now accomplished and abolished and that all believers have now most free access into heaven, where Jesus, our High Priest, whom now we see by faith in the heavens, there performing his intercession work for us, ever liveth.

Meaning what? Meaning that the Holy of Holies in the Son of man is revealed. Meaning that his altars are now manifest to all. Meaning that in his salvation there are no priestly secrets. Meaning that a child can learn his oracles. Meaning what? Meaning that just as the veil kept people from drawing near to the most holy place, so Christ, by his death, opened a way to God for himself as our blessed High Priest—and for us in him.

Meaning what? Meaning that the mysteries of the Old Testament are revealed. You must remember all along that the veil of the temple was for concealment. Except for the high priest, extremely dangerous it was for anyone to see the furniture of the most holy place within the veil. And only once a year, with great ceremony and through a cloud of smoke—all of which pointed out the darkness of that dispensation—did the high priest enter.

> *"And not as Moses, which put a vail over his face, that the children of Israel could not stedfastly look to the end of that which is abolished"*—II Cor. 3:13.

But now, at the death of Christ, "all was laid open, the mysteries unveiled, so that he that runs may read the meaning of them."

"The veil was rent." Signifying what? Signifying the uniting of Jew and Gentiles, by removing the

partition-wall between them, which partition-wall was
the ceremonial law. For by his ignominious and yet
glorious death Christ repealed that ceremonial law and
cancelled that handwriting of ordinances, nailed it to the
cross, and so "broke down the middle wall of partition."
And so Christ, by abolishing these institutions and ceremonies, by which the Jews were distinguished from all
other people, "abolished in his flesh the enmity, even the
law of commandments contained in ordinances—for to
make in himself of twain one new man," just as two
rooms are made one, by taking down the partition wall.

> *"For he is our peace, who hath made both one, and hath
> broken down the middle wall of partition between us;
> having abolished in his flesh the enmity, even the law
> of commandments contained in ordinances; for to make
> in himself of twain one new man, so making peace"*
> —EPHESIANS 2:14-15.

Meaning what? This we ask again. Meaning that the
old priesthood is superceded, that the old sacrifices have
lost their value and are absorbed in the one great sacrifice for sin. And because of this one great sacrifice for
sin, Jesus, being both High Priest and Lamb of God in
one, we say:

> *"Wherein God, willing more abundantly to shew unto
> the heirs of promise that immutability of his counsel,
> confirmed it by an oath: that by two immutable things,
> in which it was impossible for God to lie, we might
> have a strong consolation, who have fled for refuge to
> lay hold upon the hope set before us: which hope we
> have as an anchor of the soul, both sure and stedfast,
> and which entereth into that within the vail; whither
> the forerunner is for us entered, even Jesus, made an
> high priest forever after the order of Melchisedec"*
> —HEBREWS 6:17-20.

Meaning what? This once more we ask. Meaning
this—that we "have boldness to enter into the holiest by
the blood of Jesus, by a new and living way which he
hath consecrated for us, through the veil." Do we not
despair of ever answering such a charge as justice and
the law have against us? Yes, verily. We can look for
a discharge only in the blood and righteousness of Jesus.
"When Christ entered into the holiest with his blood
within the veil, he sprinkled the mercy seat, and when
the soul takes hold of this blood and righteousness of
Christ, as the ground of his acquittance from the charge
of justice, then he casts anchor within the veil."

> *"Having therefore, brethren, boldness to enter into the
> holiest by the blood of Jesus, by a new and living way,
> which he hath consecrated for us, through the vail, that
> is to say, his flesh"*—HEBREWS 10:19-20.

So we now have free access to come with boldness to a
throne of grace, to a God in Christ.

> *"Let us therefore come boldly unto the throne of grace,
> that we may obtain mercy, and find grace to help in
> time of need"*—HEBREWS 4:16.

The true holy of holies, heaven itself, is now open to
us, by the entrance of our great High Priest, that we also
may enter in by faith, as a royal priesthood, following
our great Forerunner, who for us hath entered within
the veil. So we come to the glorious truth that each believer is a priest—and we hear, with a joy ever rich and
abiding, ever fascinating and never wearisome, the
words:

> *"Grace be unto you, and peace, from him which is, and
> which was, and which is to come; and from the seven
> Spirits which are before his throne; And from Jesus*

Christ, who is the faithful witness, and the first begotten of the dead, and the prince of the kings of the earth. Unto him that loved us, and washed us from our sins in his own blood, and hath made us kings and priests unto God and his Father; to him be glory and dominion for ever and ever"—Rev. 1:4-6.

Not only was the veil of Old Testament shadows and ceremonies that interposed between God and man removed by the death of Christ, but, as a great man said years ago, there was the veil of a broken covenant, the veil of God's injured attributes, and the veil of man's sin. "By the death of Christ, the veil of a broken covenant was rent in twain, so that we might get to God through that veil of the law, for the law was fulfilled in every part of it, by his obedience to the death. Was the precept of the law a perfect obedience? Well, Christ, by his obedience to the death, did magnify the law, and make it honorable, brought in an everlasting righteousness. His death was the finishing stroke, the highest act of that obedience whereby the law was fulfilled." Was the promise of life in the law, or first covenant, forfeited by us? Well, Christ rent this veil, by redeeming the forfeiture with the price of his blood. He bought back for us the inheritance we had lost—making a purchase of us, and of eternal salvation for us. Was the penalty of death in the law standing in the way? Well, Christ comes in the sinner's room, endures the penalty, by becoming under the curse of the law, becoming obedient to the death, enduring the wrath of God—and delivering us from the wrath to come. And so, behold, the veil of a broken covenant was rent."

And—oh, 'tis wonderful—Christ, being both High Priest and Lamb of God, has gone into the presence of God in the true Holy of Holies, and hath there sprinkled his blood upon the mercy seat. Wherefore the writer of the Book of Hebrews says:

> *"But ye are come unto Mount Sion, and unto the city of the living God, the heavenly Jerusalem, and to an innumerable company of angels, to the general assembly and church of the firstborn, which are written in heaven, and to God the Judge of all and to the spirits of just men made perfect, and to Jesus the mediator of the new covenant, and to the blood of sprinkling, that speaketh better things than that of Abel. See that ye refuse not him that speaketh. For if they escaped not who refused him that spake on earth, much more shall not we escape, if we turn away from him that speaketh from heaven"*—HEBREWS 12:22-25.

And so—we could have you notice that last statement as we say, in the words of another, that since the veil is rent in twain by the death of Christ, O then come and see, come and take, come and wonder, come and enter, come and sing.

We read in Revelation the sixth chapter that when the seal was opened the voice cried, "Come and see." So, since the veil is rent, look upon this great sight, the veil of separation between God and us rent in twain from the top to the bottom. Look into the holiest and see the glorious mystery of redeeming love. Here you can see the wisdom, power, holiness, justice, goodness, and grace of God, manifested brightly in the face of Jesus who, by his death rent the veil, that we might see heaven, and the glory of it.

By Jesus' death enter boldly into the holiest. Don't stand fearfully in the outer court. Don't stand gazing. You may all come boldly to the holiest, by this new and living way that is consecrated through the veil. "O may such a dog, such a filthy dog as I come? Yes, we used to say, When doors are open, dogs come in; the door is open, the veil is rent; let dogs come in and get a crumb. The Gentiles are called dogs in Scripture! And it is said, Without are dogs, murderers, sorcerers, the licentious; but to all the dogs that are without the vail, we, in God's name, proclaim liberty to come in, and get what will *save* you and *sanctify* you. I tell you there is none here, but they have something to bring to Christ with them. What is that? Have you not much sin and misery to bring with you? Have you not much want, weakness, and wickedness, to bring with you? Come with all your ills, in order to get all good! Come with your sins, and get grace! Come with your guilt, and get a pardon! Come with your filthiness, and get cleansing! Come with your wants, and get fulness. Let dogs come in and get a crumb; yea, a feast. There is nothing to hinder you, since the veil is rent. The law is not in your way, for that is fulfilled; the flaming cherubim is not in your way, for Christ hath rent the veil of God's wrath, and divided the red-sea of divine vengeance, that you might pass through. Have you a mind for heaven, man, woman? Here is the way, it lies through the rent veil; and if you take not this way, you shall never enter there! For there are two porters that will keep all unbelievers out; namely, justice and holiness. Justice will say, I must be satisfied; holiness will say, I must be vindicated, or else you shall never enter here: but if you come by this rent veil, you shall have open entrance into the heavenly kingdom. Christ will say to justice, Let such a man in, for I paid you all his debt! Christ will say to holiness, Let such a man in, for I gave you a perfect obedience for him; look upon him in me. This will satisfy both these porters to let believers pass. O then, come and enter through the veil that is rent. Christless soul, who will satisfy justice and holiness for you? These porters will never be bribed by you. Therefore, O come, and enter by the rent veil, for there is no other way to heaven."

Come and sing. If you have made entrance, O sing, Glory to God in the highest, that ever rent this veil. You might go home singing, if you took up the true meaning of the text, and turned it to a song; and sing it with understanding, "Behold, the veil of the temple was rent in twain from the top to the bottom." Behold, the veil is rent, and shall never be whole again. Behold, the work is completed by the Son of God; the work is done, and shall never be undone. To the Author and Finisher of this great work be glory forever!

Chapter VIII

THE TWO LOVES

"Now there stood by the cross of Jesus his mother"
—John 19:25.

"But God commendeth his love toward us, in that, while we were yet sinners, Christ died for us"—Romans 5:8.

Of Jesus and Mary, *before* his birth, we read these words in Holy Writ:

"Now the birth of Jesus Christ was on this wise: When as his mother Mary was espoused to Joseph, before they came together, she was found with child of the Holy Ghost. Then Joseph, her husband, being a just man, and not willing to make her a public example, was minded to put her away privily. But while he thought on these things, behold, the angel of the Lord appeared unto him in a dream, saying, Joseph, thou son of David, fear not to take unto thee Mary thy wife: for that which is conceived in her is of the Holy Ghost. And she shall bring forth a son, and thou shalt call his name JESUS: *for he shall save his people from their sins"*
—Matt. 1:18-21.

"And Mary arose in those days, and went into the hill country with haste, into a city of Juda; and entered into the souse of Zacharias, and saluted Elizabeth. And it came to pass, that, when Elizabeth heard the salutation of Mary, the babe leaped in her womb; and Elizabeth was filled with the Holy Ghost: and she spake out with a loud voice, and said, Blessed art thou among women, and blessed is the fruit of thy womb and whence is this to me, that the mother of my Lord should come to me?"—Luke 1:39-43.

"And Mary abode with her about three months, and returned to her own house"—LUKE 1:56.

Of Jesus and Mary, *after* his birth, we read in Luke's Gospel of how the shepherds "made known abroad the saying that was told them concerning the child." And then these words:

"And all they that heard it wondered at those things which were told them by the shepherds. But Mary kept all these things, and pondered them in her heart"
—LUKE 2:18-19.

And then we read of how Simeon—"a just and devout man, waiting for the consolation of Israel, the Holy Ghost upon him"—"came by the Spirit into the temple" and there "the parents brought in the child Jesus, to do for him after the custom of the law."

"Then took he him up in his arms, and blessed God, and said, Lord, now lettest thou thy servant depart in peace, according to thy word: for mine eyes have seen thy salvation, which thou hast prepared before the face of all people; a light to lighten the Gentiles, and the glory of thy people Israel. And Joseph and his mother marvelled at those things which were spoken of him"
—LUKE 2:28-33.

During all of these days when Mary was in more perplexity than any woman ever was since Eve, this old saint, named Simeon, seeing and holding in his arms the only babe who had no earthly father, sang a great song. And there was one deep minor note in that song that pierced Mary's heart, even as later the cruel spike pierced Mary's son. That deep minor note is found in these words: "A sword shall pierce through thine own soul also."

Mary never forgot those words. They were with her when the sun rose and when the sun went down. They were with her in her waking hours. They were with her —disturbing her no doubt—in her dreams. Sometimes she thought the day birds sang sadly and that the night birds sang weirdly of that sword. Sometimes when quivering lightning split the clouds that gathered above the hills around Nazareth, she thought she saw the sword—the sword in the soul. Sometimes when the moon blossomed like a huge jonquil in the garden of the stars, she thought she saw that sword amid the shadows in the moonlight. But she did not know all that Simeon meant until that day when she saw Jesus naked and dying upon the Cross. And that dark and tragic day the prophetic sword of Simeon did pierce through her soul.

"There stood by the cross of Jesus his mother." Of course, she did. Where else could any mother like the mother Mary was stand on such a day? Parting and pain, sorrow and suffering, darkness and earthquake, hooting mouths and wagging heads, rattling dice and dripping blood—"there stood by the cross of Jesus his mother." There we see a *mother's* love. Yes, a mother's love manifesting itself where God was proving his love to sinners.

The love of Jesus' mother followed him to the crest of Calvary—in spite of the fact that, so far as the world was concerned, he was a criminal and an outcast—despised and rejected of men—hated and hooted, spat upon, derided and desecrated, scorned and sneered at. It is easy enough to love a man when everyone else loves him —or when everything goes well and everybody speaks kindly of him. It is easy enough to love a man or woman when society eulogizes him. But the real test of a woman's love is when the crucifixion of shame and regret and failure and dishonor come. Like most mothers, thank God, the mother of Jesus stood the test and stuck to him until the end. In so doing, she herself suffered as he suffered. The mother of Jesus partook of the bitter gall in the lifted cup of hate. The mother of Jesus felt on her brow the biting puncturing of the cruel thorns. The mother of Jesus felt the nails driven in her own hands. The mother of Jesus felt the spikes in her own feet as they were driven into the feet of her son. The mother of Jesus felt also the spear-thrust in her own side as the soldier flung his spear into the Master's side. The mother of Jesus cried out in her soul, too: "My God, my God, why hast thou forsaken me?" But she lingered with him till the last.

Let us think a bit on the love of mothers—if you will.

"Many daughters have done virtuously, but thou excellest them all"—PROVERBS 31:29.

Thus the author of Proverbs gives mothers and motherhood the highest place in the civilization of his day. And if we serve God rightly, we must give motherhood a high place in the age in which we live—motherhood and motherhood love. "If the wolves of rapine and hate, ever hungry and dangerous, are howling at the door of our civilization, we must bring forth the teachings— kind, simple, noble, true—taught us by Christian mothers and practice them as a mighty force to save us from wrong directions and tragic disaster."

I think it was Dr. J. B. Baker who has told us that among God's creatures there is none in whom the ardor of affection is so tropically warm as in a mother. "The warm blood of her heart sends life into the form of her unborn child, the warm press of her lips sends healing into the wounds of her bruised child, the warm breath of her soul sends thoughts into the mind of her plastic child, the warm beam of her eyes sends cheer into the face of her bearded son. Through childhood and maturity she is the one unfailing sanatorium of all the cold world's bitterest ailments. What she does is neither scientific nor philanthropic, as the records of men are kept, but she reaches suffering that the philanthropists never dream of and heals diseases that the scientist can not touch."

Talmadge used to say that when the two Wesleys—John and Charles—approach their throne in heaven they will find one in the middle, higher than either, for mother.

It gives us joy to know that no sin is great enough to quench the love of mother. Her heart is a fountain that never runs dry. We are told that Sir Walter Scott had a brother Dan, who taxed his mother's constancy more than William Penn. He was the black sheep of the flock, who ruined himself financially and morally through the acquaintance of dissolute women. So great was the dishonor that he brought upon the family name that Sir Walter neither attended the funeral nor wore mourning for him—and when he spoke of him, he refused to own him as a brother—and referred to him as a relative. But the mother of the boys was not so. No mother ever was. "Her arms, like the branch of the generous oak, are open for the recreant as well as the upright." We see many mother's proving this every day by their ceaseless tread to the court house and to the jail. Mother love is as fathomless as the sea, as immeasurable as the heavens, as unweighable as mountains in an apothecary's scales.

Years ago in Georgia and South Carolina **criminals**, for certain crimes, when found guilty by a jury of twelve men, were often sentenced to be hanged on a public gallows before the eyes of any and all who cared to witness such a gruesome spectacle. The condemned man was made to sit on his own coffin in a wagon—and the wagon was driven out through the streets to a public hanging place where, with a black hood for the face and a strong rope for the neck, the sentence of death was carried out. Once Frank Stanton, the great Southern poet, saw these scenes—saw them all—death wagon and coffin and the condemned man and the gallows and the death. And that day he wrote:

> *"That's him there on his coffin in the cart,*
> *And there in the crowd is a woman creeping,*
> *Yes, there in the crowd is a woman weeping—*
> *And the law is just a-breakin' of her heart.*

> *"That's him there on the scaffold. See! He speaks.*
> *And there is a woman a-holding*
> *Of the hands they'll soon be folding—*
> *And the tears are just a-raining down her cheeks.*

> *"That's him there on his coffin—lyin' low,*
> *And a woman—the first of all to love him,*
> *Yes, a woman—the last to bend above him*
> *Is his mother! But I guess that you would know."*

But if we could put all the sweet mother love that has ever been in all mother hearts into one heart and let it beat for years and years, we could not express as much love as did God manifest to sinners during those hours when Jesus made his body and his sinless soul an offering for our sins. God's love to sinners is above and beyond all love as a river is beyond a rill in reach, as the sun is beyond a tallow dip in brightness, as a tree is beyond a twig in fruit bearing, as the wings of an eagle are beyond the feet of a snail in swiftness, as an ocean is beyond a mud-hole in depth, as a mountain is beyond a cave in lofty grandeur, as the perfume of flowers is beyond the odors of a garbage can, as the glories of a dawn are beyond the gaudy stage lights. What depths beyond all fathoming in his love! What heights beyond all climbing in his love! What expanse beyond all measuring in his love! What beauty beyond all describing, what sweetness beyond all bitterness in his love!

Back of and undergirding and crowning with glory Bethlehem's barn, where Mary held in her arms the babe who had no earthly father, was God's love. For the incarnation of God in Christ was born of prompting love in the heart of God. This mysterious and marvelous means for the rescue of man, testifying to God's omniscient and omnipotent resourcefulness in facing the tragedies caused by sin, the causative element of all world woes, was born in God's holy heart of holy love. Back of and under and around and above the Cross is the love of God, for only at the Cross is the history of divine love made intelligible. There the love that had waited for ages in whispering silence, spoke with a voice and in a language that all the world could hear. There love, in crimson garments dressed, courted man's love— laid siege at the heart of man, with atoning pleading. There love, placing a priceless value on the soul of man, counted no sacrifice too great to prove God's love, unsealed the fountain of salvation and solved the problem of human redemption. There God showed not only the deep of man's sin but the deep of his own love. For there, with a love deeper than sin, "he bare our sins in his own body on the tree" (I Peter 2:24).

God's love is longer than the longest road—longer than the longest night of agony—longer than the longest day of sorrow—longer than the longest trial of affliction. "I have loved thee with an everlasting love" (Jer. 31:3).

> *"He loved me, ere yet one ray of light*
> *Had flashed across the boundless sky!*
> *He loved me then: and shall it ever die?"*

> *"Ah, no, that love shall onward, onward roll,*
> *Increasing in its flow, till like the sea,*
> *It breaks in thrills of rapture on the soul,*
> *And spends itself through all eternity."*

As my friend, Dr. Moyer says: "A sinner may go to hell *unsaved;* he can not go to hell *unloved.*"

> *"His love no end nor measure knows,*
> *No change can turn its course,*
> *Eternally the same it flows*
> *From one eternal source."*

"What shall we then say to these things? If God be for us, who can be against us? He that spared not his own Son, but delivered him up for us all, how shall he not with him also freely give us all things? Who shall lay anything to the charge of God's elect? It is God that justifieth. Who is he that condemneth? It is Christ that died, yea rather, that is risen again, who is even at the right hand of God, who also maketh intercession for us. Who shall separate us from the love of Christ? shall tribulation, or distress, or persecution, or famine, or nakedness, or peril, or sword? As it is written, For thy sake we are killed all the day long; we are accounted as sheep for the slaughter. Nay, in all these things we are more than conquerors through him that

*loved us. For I am persuaded, that neither death, nor
life, nor angels, nor principalities, nor powers, nor
things present, nor things to come, nor height, nor
depth, nor any other cerature, shall be able to separate
us from the love of God, which is in Christ Jesus our
Lord"*—ROMANS 8:31-39.

All of which makes us write what Robert Moyer, quoting
another, has beautifully written:

"As we gaze upon the cross the whole being of Christ
speaks with substitutionary love—and the whole environment is replete with vicarious suffering! His heart of
love bleeds in death to cleanse us. His hands of love are
wounded to heal us. His feet of love are nailed to
release us. His side of love is pierced to assure us. His
body of love is stripped to clothe us. His lips of love
are parched to bless us. His tongue of love is agonized
to calm us. His head of love is cursed with thorns to
crown us. His cross of love is shameful to enrich us.
His death of love is awful to quicken us.

"The whole surroundings of the cross throb with love.
The darkened heavens are bright with love's joy. The
rending rocks are opened with love's grace. The cruel
tree is blooming with love's fruit. The hate of man is
the dark background for love's action. The malice of
hell is the opportunity for love's triumph. The mocking
of the crowd is the call for love's patience. And the
suffering for sin unfolds the provision of love's grace."

The two loves!

Mother love!

> *"O, mother, when I think of thee,
> 'Tis but a step to Calvary."*

God's love!

At the cross, beholding him who never sinned dying

for sinners, beholding him who had no sin *in* him and yet had all sin *on* him, can we hug our lives close, withholding from the altar, and—when the bugles of duty summon to service—ourselves from the arena? God forbid. Shall we not the rather, looking upon that cross, respond sacrificially and heroically to the marching orders of his kingdom's great advance? Shall we not the rather, taking counsel no more of our fears, living no longer on the fringes, content no more to toss about in the offing, that his way may be known upon the earth, his saving health among all nations, let him have his way with us?

> *"Child of sin and sorrow,*
>   *Filled with dismay,*
> *Wait not for tomorrow,*
>   *Yield thee today:*
> *Heaven bids thee come,*
>   *While yet there's room:*
> *Child of sin and sorrow,*
>   *Hear and obey.*
>
> *"Child of sin and sorrow,*
>   *Why wilt thou die?*
> *Come while thou canst borrow*
>   *Help from on high;*
> *Grieve not that love*
>   *Which from above,*
> *Child of sin and sorrow,*
>   *Would bring thee nigh."*